SHORTCUT TO HAVING MORE

YOUR WEALTH BLUEPRINT

SASHA JAMES

All Rights Reserved 2017 @POWER of ONE

Table of Contents

INTRODUCTION 7
   WHY THIS BOOK? 7
   WHAT to EXPECT 11
   BLOCKS & OBSTACLES 15
   NEVER TOO LATE FOR THE REAL THING 23
SIGNIFICANCE OF (UNDERSTANDING) MONEY 28
SIGNIFICANCE OF (PRECIOUS) TIME 34
UPPER FLOORS VERSUS THE 'RAT RACE' OF THE UNDERGROUND LEVEL 38
   BEGINNING OF INTERACTIVE MEDITATION ->>> 41
   <<<- END OF INTERACTIVE MEDITATION. 49
EVER EXPANDING 51
PART I 53
   STRUGGLING THROUGH A NEW BEGINNING 53
'AHA' (Or, There IS an Elevator) Moment 59
PART II 65
   ORIGINS & BASICS 65
   ONE but DIFFERENT 74

ABOVE the MIND 79

FREE WILL 82

PEELING THE ONION... 87

PART III. 93

THE TRUTH ABOUT MONEY..................................... 93

COUNTER-INTENTIONS.. 97

DEVASTATING NATURE OF COUNTER-INTENTIONS 104

Part IV. 113

METHOD EXPLAINED 113

CONNECTING TO THE SOURCE 113

Two Source Energy Centers................................. 116

A few things before you start:............................. 121

GUIDED EXERCISE - CONNECTING TO THE SOURCE ENERGY.. 122

YOUR PERSONAL WEALTH BLUEPRINT........................ 129

Introduction.. 129

FIVE TYPES OF MONEY 135

FIVE TYPES OF MONEY - MAPPING EXERCISE..... 139

Personal Wealth Blueprint Tapping Script 167

CLEARING.. 169

Preparation... 169

DIGGING ROUND 182

POSITIVE ROUND 192

Personal Wealth Blueprint Tapping Script 199

CONCLUDING WORDS 202
  Reality Check 205
All Rights Reserved 2017 @POWER of ONE 212

INTRODUCTION

WHY THIS BOOK?

Let me start by answering this 'why' question with a few short lines, just in case you (like me) have a habit of making decisions based on quickly skimming initial paragraphs: 'I'll read this now, later or never.' In that case, my reason sounds something like this: *"I have compiled this book in order to assist sincere men and women to efficiently remove all obstacles that slow or block their ability of earning more, having more, and becoming more."* These methods mean so much to me and to everyone who takes this process seriously.

Over the last few years, I have gathered many direct experiences leading to crystal-clear evidence of the significant changes made in others' lives by the *'Shortcut to Having More'* methods. Nothing else could give me more happiness than seeing clients' lives changed in so many aspects with those significant leaps forward. I could also answer this question by simply saying: "BECAUSE IT WORKS." However, this is an even better answer: "You should give it a try because it provides you with a fluff-free, effective method including helpful tools. It offers tangible results to everyone who is willing to think out-of-the-box. It simply changes so much in the lives of every individual ready to face and deal with the root of his (or her) problems."

On that note, let me explain some history.

At the high point of my career, about two decades ago, my life went from (as I perceived it) a great level of success and lifestyle (high level of income, booming business, luxurious cars, house, exclusive vacations, etc) to the point of finding myself owning nothing. Practically speaking, I was left without any money or material possessions. With about $450 in my pocket, I had to find a way for me and my family to survive in the next month. This drastic and sudden change happened to us incredibly fast, without involving fast women, cars, drugs, or a gambling addiction – none of those types of fall-off-a-cliff reasons. I had been managing an IT business, and held a majority-level number of shares in a company that owned 80% of a 32 million-person market share that consisted of six countries in the Eastern European region. [Further details will be available in my next book – I don't want to derail the focus from our very important work in exploring ways to have more and be more.]

Once I managed to stop lamenting, the understanding was born for the first time - I HAVE to change in order to HAVE MORE and BECOME MORE. So, I started to read and listen to everything that (I hoped) could help me grow. Naturally, I have learned a lot while also facing another reality; many times, I have felt betrayed and frustrated on that road. After reading and trying to follow the advice of various teachers, so-called "gurus" and experts, I can say honestly that the general concepts were very helpful - except when it came to specifics. Many of you have had similar (and rather bitter) experiences.

When it came to any practical application of 'how exactly/what exactly/when exactly do I do what' in order to grow and move quickly toward my goals, I have hit wall after wall. No, I wasn't jumping from book to book and from program to program. Really, I honestly tried with my full concentration to follow the books and programs to their conclusion. Yes, I was digging through various books, programs and other materials, searching for answers in categories related to personal development: the Law of Attraction, personal transformation, *Think & Grow Rich* related approaches, energy work, hypnosis, clearing limiting beliefs, and on and on. Only after giving it a good solid try did I move on after each approach, mainly because I wasn't getting a desired (or most often, a promised and strongly marketed) batch of results. But, something did work. That something, as I see it, most people fail to even recognize. It is not strongly advertised; no ads will wave it in front of our faces or dangle it in front of our noses.

In any case, based on that experience, *I strongly feel* that it is a fair, healthy, and necessary thing to openly disclose what this book is really about.

WHAT to EXPECT

To give you a clear idea, let's review the words used in the title. That will help you decide whether this approach is something that resonates with you and your goal.

'SHORTCUT'*:* A shortcut is a way of getting to the desired destination faster without the risk of losing anything. A shortcut may help you to achieve what you really want without spending too much time or effort…getting there without wandering, confusion, hassle, or danger.

'HAVING MORE': We all want to have more of 'something,' but we often have less than we want of that something. For many people, *Having More* in this book and its title may only indicate *more money,* which is quite accurate. Earning more money IS one of the first big milestones of this process, and almost everyone pursues it. At the same time, as soon as wealth begins to manifest, one realizes this process of *Having More* means a lot more than 'earning more money'. In its fullness, this concept of *Having More* will powerfully influence the quality of our relationships, emotions, social interactions, and other aspects of life.

Yes, it is true that more money, wealth, and prosperity is in sight; we (most of us humans on the planet) are driven by these things. However, it really transforms the quality of our existence on practically all levels where we desire *to have, feel, own,* and *live more.* Now, what people plan on doing with their money can differ greatly from person to person — for that reason, 'success' or 'wealth' or even 'earning a lot' is an individual definition. Regardless, it does involve earning and keeping *more money* and *more success.* Ultimately, 'Having More' is actually *a transition into something better* and *becoming more.*

ULTIMATELY, A '*SHORTCUT TO HAVING MORE*' PROVIDES YOU WITH TOOLS FOR REMOVING BLOCKS AND OBSTACLES ON YOUR PATH TO EVOLVING INTO THE BEST VERSION OF YOURSELF.

Before we can start removing a stumbling block, we must learn what it is and how it can be removed. One of the beginning points of this 'Having More' method is the creation of your *Personal Wealth Blueprint*; this mapped strategy identifies your obstacles and blockages and then offers an exact method for you to successfully clear those obstacles from your system. You will gain new power—the power of clarity to see what is slowing you down. The *Personal Wealth Blueprint* is a fantastic way to help you detect and eliminate blocks that have slowed you down for 10, 20, or even over 30 years, depending on your age. Let me share with you the characteristics of this method, what it is and what it is not.

> It is NOT a THEORETICAL APPROACH. In front of you is something not merely about reading but about <u>applying</u>. If you are **only** in pursuit of entertainment and *acquiring a theoretical understanding* about something that might help–you can move on, this isn't for you. If adding a book to your dust collection and arsenal of 'cool stuff' sounds like a good idea, this book is not for you.

- It WORKS in a PRACTICAL WAY: This content is for action takers. Naturally, we can doubt anything (doubt being a sign of intelligence), which is perfectly fine. However, if one does not give this approach a chance, how can one decide whether or not it is worthwhile?

- It is PERSONALIZED: As individual spiritual entities, we all come into this world with different varieties of baggage. All of us share common principles and points of reference; on the other hand, we are also different. These methods and applications, as presented, are customizable to individual needs and desires without sacrificing the effectiveness of the process, which starts with the creation of your *Personal Wealth Blueprint.*

- It saves TIME, ENERGY, AND EFFORT: This is for people who respect time and do not like to waste it. Regardless of how many systems you have already tried, the methods presented here will empower and help you, not only to expand your earning ability, but also provide you with the power to manifest the reality that you desire without spending huge amounts of time or costing you a fortune.

- CRYSTAL CLEAR: Some people do not like a solid framework of instructions. Others, however, get incredible value from following practices that are defined and proven to deliver results. This approach will provide you with clear advice, instructions, and recommendations about everything covered in this book.

BLOCKS & OBSTACLES

Without anything to stop us (i.e. without carrying inside a program that makes us live with the parking brake on), and if we were not held back by various subconscious blocks and beliefs, each and every one of us would already be earning our desired amount of wealth. Our lives would look and feel a lot different than they do now—especially if our bank accounts held all of the money we desired! The existence of these blocks, those things that keep us from **having more,** is not anything new or unknown. These days, you can read a lot about overcoming restrictive beliefs and subconscious blocks; however, rarely is there an approach specific and potent enough to penetrate to the root of each unwanted influence we carry within ourselves. For this reason, I will list some examples of influences that can restrict individuals from achieving their monetary dreams or other forms of success. Some of these may sound relevant to you while others may not; however, I would like to assure you that all of them are important and need your attention. This is why:

MANY PEOPLE SPEAK ABOUT BLOCKS AND OBSTACLES ON OUR PATH TO SUCCESS (LIMITING BELIEFS, SELF-SABOTAGE, AND COUNTER-INTENTIONS), BUT WE WILL TEACH YOU HOW TO DETECT AND ELIMINATE THEM ONCE FOR ALL!

Truthfully, clearing up some of these complicated barriers will require a lot of time and attention, while some of the simpler obstacles will take less time. It depends on which barriers lie on your road to success. In later chapters of this book, we will create your *Personal Wealth Blueprint*, an exercise that individually addresses wealth and money issues for every person who applies the process. Once you apply the *Personal Wealth Blueprint* as offered in the second half of this book, you will see the exact nature of those obstacles that slow you down. More importantly, the '*Shortcut to Having More*' methods, as described in this work and the other works in the series, will assist you in successfully dealing with all of your (financial) issues. Below is a summary of different unwanted elements that are limiting your subconscious and conscious mind, so you can identify your own limits, and be on your way toward doubling and tripling your earning potential within the next 12 months.

Embarrassment and Shame: Most often, these hidden and deep-rooted emotions are manifested in self-punishment and self-pity. Most of the time we are not aware of this one at all!

***Resistance to Change*:** Theoretically, we would like change, but a protection system inside of us slows down the process. It uses certain phrases as a mask. "Change = danger." "Just stay like you are now, that is safe."

Clearing Self-doubt: Once you become aware of fears and self-doubts, and become equipped with powerful tools (as explained later), you will feel extremely empowered.

Fear(s): Many people (especially men) have a hard time recognizing their fear or fears. That does not change the fact that if we maintain our subconscious fear, we cannot grow our potential for earning, creating, and keeping more money. These are some of the most common fears:

- Fear of Change
- Fear of Failure
- Fear of Scarcity
- Fear of Success
- Fear of Rejection

Once these fears have been detected, using a customized blueprint provided at the beginning of the Practical section of this book, and then treated properly (using methods presented later on), these fears will be shifted and then cleared out of our subconscious minds and programmed behavioral systems.

Take hold of the tools that allow you to shape, grow, and cultivate your own wealth in any direction you can imagine. You will clear away the baggage and break free from the old restrictions that have sucked out energy from you.

Family blocks: Many of the blocks listed here are related to our families, parents, or caregivers in our early childhood. However, sometimes there are very specific and subconscious emotions connected to family that needs our special attention, as well as additional work, in order to get cleared. Many people are not in the process of achieving even 10% of what they could easily do because of a desire to avoid "trying to be better" than their father, mother, etc.

Blame: This is definitely a big block. Locating the

blame-related patterns and programs is an essential step; otherwise, learners get diverted or re-routed from their path. Once the patterns are clearly detected, we can dig for the roots and destroy these obstacles.

Self-sabotage: Everything on this list is a form of self-sabotage related to the mind and body. However, many of us hold specific deep-rooted and subconscious programs and belief patterns. They can become auto-triggered at any time, as soon as we have a chance to earn more money, achieve success, get a better-paying job, apply for something that generates a higher income, etc. These revealed processes of body, mind, money, tools, and approaches will give you everything that you need to liberate yourself into empowerment, discover the *secret energy of having more,* and how to tap into it.

Self-worth: Again, this type of block is not sensed on a conscious level. Most of us have to learn ways in which the love we received as a child currently influences our earning potential and bank account. In this process, we successfully deal with residual influences, learn how to create powerful money channels, and fill ourselves with true and genuine self-love.

False expectations and illusions: These are quite popular blocks on our path of *having more*, especially among the think-big facilitators of the Law of Attraction or mind reprogramming who push people to set (unrealistic) million-dollar goals. Some people get rid of these blocks without much trouble, while some have really deep work to do in these areas. Regardless, if one allows these expectations and illusions to grow and blossom, they turn into specific obstacles that sabotage any ability to move forward and to achieve. They can definitely keep us from generating a higher income level and becoming financially <u>free</u> in the real sense of the word. If these obstacles are present in your life, we can discover them and detect the exact reasons for their appearance. Their disappearance will result in a fast transmutation toward our ability to accept big goals and big dreams that realistically align with our energy and real selves.

"I don't know ...": This barrier really hits a lot of people in a few different forms.

- I don't know what I really want.
- I don't know what I really have to do.
- I don't know if I want to change.
- I don't know if I want to change at all.

Basically, it's a big lie. All of us are very clear about what we have to do, as well as our best direction for growth. However, people do face this block to growth; sometimes, people will remain stuck with it for the rest of their lives.

Of course, everyone has more blocks and programmed beliefs roaming through their subconscious and conscious minds. However, this list will give you a fairly clear idea about what you can expect to get out of this book and this approach. Most importantly, I want to promise you one thing–although, granted, I don't know you personally. I don't know the details of your situation; I don't know the severity of your karma and the amount of baggage that you carry. But I can, and I want to, *promise you* this:

All of these obstacles *(and programmed self-talk patterns, etc.) that stop you from moving out of where you are right now to where you want to be****, can and will be cleared****; they will be* ***deleted*** *from your system, provided that you enlarge your* ***awareness*** *and give this approach a chance.*

NEVER TOO LATE FOR THE REAL THING

Those of you who are not new to the path of personal development and self-discovery, you have already survived experiences of struggle and pain, failure and disappointment. I know how confusing that is, and how hard that feels. At the same time, I know how revealing and sweet it is to be freed from all of that burden! It's not only about my own experience, but also about seeing the identical results appear in the lives of people I have shared this with, such as friends and clients who I work with one-on-one. Again, using the same words in just a few previous paragraphs, this is my answer to the legitimate question, "Why have you decided to write down this approach?"

BECAUSE IT FREAKING WORKS.

If you want to make it work, it will. This method is easy to understand and apply, while it delivers significant improvements and rapid long-lasting results.

Also, that's the other reason why I didn't write this book earlier—because writing is not my main area of expertise. The actual idea of putting everything into a digestible form of a short and practical book was presented to me by the very people whose lives had been transformed with the help of this approach. For a few years, I heard this idea of 'publish a book/put all of this in the book' *before* I understood the value of that good advice.

It's strange, in a way, because I love helping others…I really enjoy seeing others become free of pain, fear, and scarcity. For quite a while, I have seen that task, of assisting others on the path of growth and self-discovery, as the most important part of my existence. Therefore, the decision to create this book felt so good and right as soon as it was made. Time and time again, I have witnessed people drastically change their financial situation, which practically transforms their whole lives. Those are the sweetest moments—when my client finally 'gets it', when it clicks and he (or she) starts experiencing the results of the *'Shortcut to Having More'* methods. I'm convinced that this book can help you achieve the same results in your life. I'm sure it will assist you toward becoming the best version of yourself in a practical and specific way.

I do not know you personally, but I know this very well. These methods will give you a total makeover of your ability to earn and keep money. You will be able to achieve much more, have a lot more fun, and feel far better with your new ability to create more money, wealth, and prosperity.

If you would like me to summarize the specifics, these methods will be disclosed within the '*Shortcut to Having More*'. Overall, this is what they will do:

- HELP you understand why you are <u>not earning</u> the amount of money you really deserve to earn.

- PINPOINT specific money blocks, programmed self-talk patterns, and obstacles that force you to stay in a stunted state (i.e. in survival rather than in growth mode).

- Empower you, once and for all, to clear the obstacles from the conscious and subconscious parts of your mind.

- MAKE YOU FEEL lighter with more energy, clarity, enthusiasm, and fun.

- ASSIST you to deal with deeply rooted issues in the most efficient way.

As a result, you will...

- BECOME EMPOWERED to double or triple your earning potential within a truly short time.

- UNCOVER the true reason you don't have enough/earn enough.

- LEARN how to free yourself of this pattern quickly and easily.

- EXPERIENCE a true internal shift in your confidence, inner sense of value, and beliefs about what is truly possible for you to be, do, and have.

- ACCELERATE your achievement of greater wealth by unleashing your natural brilliance, passion, enthusiasm, and energy.

- EXPAND into who you really are.

- GROW into the best version of yourself.

SIGNIFICANCE OF (UNDERSTANDING) MONEY

What is money, in the first place? Why are there so many associated emotions, from pain and struggle to excitement and joy? Why is everything placed in relation to money?

So many people are confused; they don't see the real nature of money. The biggest mistake people make is to consider the material aspect of money and finances as an all-encompassing package—all in all. Without understanding the inner nature of money and wealth, people become trapped in scarcity consciousness. Within the four walls of scarcity, one believes the Big Pie Theory in this universe (or the Zero Sum Fallacy in economics): "There is not enough for everyone." Greed, fear, and anxiety become the dominant emotions that drive and direct their lives. As a result, gathering money, piling up things, and having more than their neighbors can become an obsession; in this way, the material aspect of money becomes the ultimate goal of existence. As a result, people suffer so much—nothing good comes out of this approach to money and wealth. Love of money, in this way, makes people waste their time and life!

MONEY CANNOT BE A SATISFACTORY LIFE GOAL FOR ANY INTELLIGENT MAN OR WOMAN.

If you do not fully understand why I'm saying this, that may be the exact cause of your overall financial lack: not earning enough money, not having enough money in your savings account, not having enough successful or productive investments, etc. For that reason, let me explain a little bit more about this, without going into too much philosophical detail. The spiritual aspect of money is of the **greatest importance**. One can understand it as a creative force, a type of energy of creation, a tool of expression that humans can master. Our relationship with money *directly resembles our inner state of development*.

We move through our path in life, looking for pleasure, happiness (or anything) that can satisfy those urges we feel, screaming from the depth of our hearts. In some way or another, that inner voice is always connected with having money, wealth, and prosperity. Most people understand this fact more often than not, yet some individuals are unable to perceive that connection. Let's be honest and clear about that. *Why is money perceived to be so important in the first place?* Why should earning, making, and keeping money have such a great influence on practically each and every aspect of our lives? Thousands of books, programs, television shows, and movies deal with this topic. As you know, we could spend huge amounts of time on this topic alone, but I have good news:

In order to get rid of everything that stops us from earning two, three, or even ten times the amount of income you have now, you **do not need** an extensive understanding of finances or the financial world (provided that knowledge isn't necessary to provide greater value to your clients).

All of us, however, need efficient methods to clear those blocks and obstacles to 'having more'; most of those methods are kept within ourselves unconsciously. This is the whole topic of this book; you will most certainly receive all you need in order to be successful in clearing the path to greatness.

So, we've circled back to the first question. Really, what is money? Are we speaking about pieces of paper, printed green in United States, blue and orange in Spain, purple and red in Canada, and a whole rainbow of colors in other countries? Is money really only paper labeled with different numbers, in ones and zeros? Again, without diving too deeply, I would like to summarize just a few conclusions that can be greatly beneficial and offer help to everyone on this path.

- Money is only a representation and a carrier of value; it is not the goal of life but rather a channel and tool for value exchange. Another way to say this is a proverb: 'Money is a wonderful servant but a bad master.'

- Collecting and having money cannot be the end goal of (intelligent) human life, but it is definitely a great tool to help us achieve our goals while living a full life.

- Having a lot of money without applying inner work doesn't give anyone their desired results; truly, it does not make anyone really abundant, wealthy, and happy.

- External manifestations of 'being rich' are often deceptive and of a flickering, temporary nature. Without living in harmony, without having an understanding of 'having more', nothing can carry us to the stage of real satisfaction and fulfillment.

SIGNIFICANCE OF (PRECIOUS) TIME

All of us take different life paths, even if they appear similar, trying to figure out the meaning and significance of our own existence. Time plays a naturally significant role. Our search for how to get more from life, enjoy more happiness, more fulfillment, deeper spiritual connection or material success...all of these things bring us to a *path of growing*. We label that path by certain names: personal development, professional growth, spirituality, life mission, etc. However, that label is not at all important. What is really important is what we get from the path that we decide to follow – the types of advancement and tangible, real results we receive as a result of following the path we have chosen.

Again, another crucial factor is time. If your thinking is similar to mine, one very important aspect of any one our goals is speed - *how fast we achieve those results*. What is the use of achieving or completing my goals if that does not leave me enough time to actually live?

"All good things take time…" This phrase gets repeated to us endlessly, but we also know that when something doesn't feel smooth, when something feels like too much endeavor, it probably *isn't* the best way. Sometimes we need the school of hard knocks; sometimes we need to feel some pain. I agree with that, but we should *never* need to use this method as a way of spending our most precious asset, the most valuable currency that we possess or process—our time.

Let me ask you one thing: *Based on your experience, can there BE a shortcut?*

In other words, can we find a method that provides not only knowledge, but also (most importantly) practical tools that can save us a lot of time and effort on our journey of **searching** *for something that doesn't just make sense but actually works?*

In my experience, the answer is the biggest Y-E-S you can imagine!

How can I be that positive about it? Well, it did require a *freaking* long journey for me. I was traveling all around a convoluted, meandering back road, missing the point by hundreds of miles and failing to see the signposts to the shortcut. In fact, I think that I took the *longest path of trial and error* that exists. Trust me, I am grateful for every second spent on that road. For me, that school of hard knocks was needed for some reason. For a long time, I had no idea what that reason was, but as soon I started to think of assisting and helping others on this path, a whole new dimension unrolled. All of that pain and struggle that I went through now gives me great power and strength to reach out and help anyone who is ready. I genuinely dislike seeing others suffering or in pain, especially when I can do something about it.

Perhaps I always knew that all of the difficulties and pain points were part of my reality for a reason. It wasn't easy to acknowledge that while suffering and getting poor (or nonexistent) results.

Time may be an illusion—certainly some esoteric people and quantum physicists explain this idea elaborately—but in this dimension, most of us consider the time factor as our greatest treasure.

I respect each and every second that I have, and I know you do as well; for that reason, I am positive that you will hear me out. You can save great swaths of time, an incredible amount of precious energy, by learning from my mistakes or by simply absorbing the methods and approaches in this book.

UPPER FLOORS VERSUS THE 'RAT RACE' OF THE UNDERGROUND LEVEL

I always knew *there must be an easier way*. There had to be a shortcut to a better life! Some of you may feel similarly. Some of you don't, but this is probably the crucial point of your decision. It's simple, actually—even if you have a closed mind or you think that any advancement in earning money *must* be hard work, I humbly request that you give this chapter a chance. A last chance, if you decide to do so.

From experience with my clients, I know that many people feel very positively about getting to a much better and faster way—but along the way, many do give up. Some give up more quickly while others give up after a long time of trying hard; in any case, I understand that response. A few times, I was just one thin thread away from giving up; I know the feeling of walking the tightrope of life. As explained, taking a shortcut to a 'Having More' state of mind does not involve losing anything or compromising the quality of anything on the path. If you are not in the mood for the upcoming story/exercise, please let me share its conclusion with the hope that you will later return to the story and explanation.

ON THE JOURNEY FROM THE GROUND TO THE TOP FLOOR, YOU CAN CLIMB BY STAIRS...OR, IF YOU KNOW HOW, SIMPLY TAKE THE ELEVATOR.

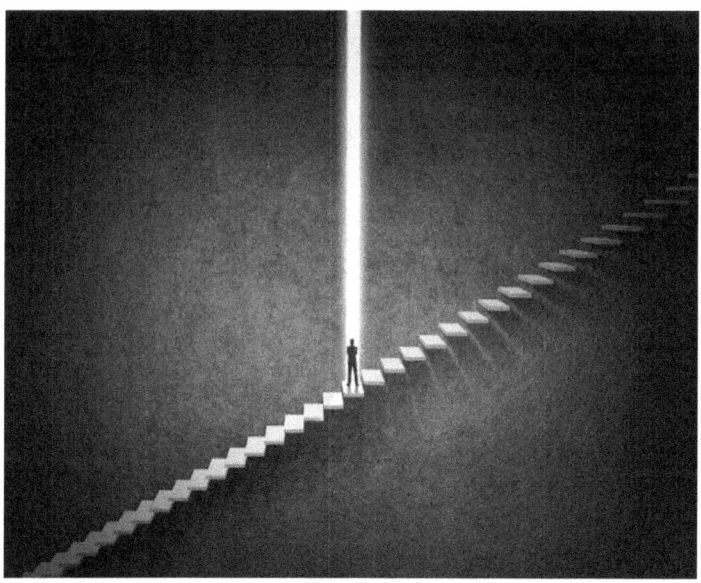

Let's dive a little bit deeper with something that is very simple and easy to do. This interactive meditation exercise functions on several levels; while it's not the most important part of any soul-searching method, it is very helpful. I am quite sure you haven't already experienced this approach to digging deeper. If you have time to peacefully read through the next five minutes, let's do it.

Take a breath, lean back for a minute, and imagine an empty movie screen in front of your eyes. Since you are reading and not listening to my voice, this cannot be a guided meditation. However, your mind is creative and you still have the ability to create pictures while reading.

Paint the following image on the screen of your mind in as much detail as you can. If you can, it's best to imagine yourself right there in the following situations. Try to see everything through the eyes of a participant. The more detail you are able to create within your mind, the stronger and better results you will achieve from this simple exercise. Read and do your best to 'be there':

BEGINNING OF INTERACTIVE MEDITATION ->>>

You're walking across town on a peaceful, sunny afternoon. All of a sudden, you find yourself in front of a building that you never noticed before. In moving closer, you realize that this is some sort of incredibly opulent, impressive, 230-floor building. You look up and can hardly see the top of the building as it reaches an incredibly high level. Walking toward the entrance, you can see that the building is not only high but also unusually big–it covers several blocks– and seems incredibly interesting; it's definitely something you want to check out. While entering one of the magnificent marble corridors, you cannot stop wondering about the luxurious, opulent detail of this building. Inside, the place is filled with people weaving in and out and around the place. Everyone seems to be busy, and the reception desk has a line of people waiting to be served. You're interested to learn more because, for some reason, this building and everything inside looks very familiar to you. It is slightly irritating, a nagging feeling, but you feel eager to discover a reason for it. You keep walking around the ground floor, looking around the lavish space, exploring. There are conference rooms, shops, cinemas, health and fitness centers, luxury stores with watches and jewelry, as well as displays of famous fashion brands. Despite that, everything seems to be happening somewhere else, not here on the ground floor.

Although the space is really gorgeous and bathed in enticing light, you become restless - your mind starts to feel overwhelmed by all these incredible luxurious facilities you're seeing all around the ground floor. You start thinking about the deeper meaning of this place and these stylishly decorated red-and-white marble corridors, gold, precious stones, and Persian carpets; they seem to be hiding something much more valuable. As you start searching for answers, you start noticing written messages placed around the walls, around the ground floor, and its corridors. While reading, you recognize different messages hanging from various locations, and read them one by one. Each and every message sounds familiar. Each message is meant to apply to you and your current situation—directing and inspiring you toward improvement, betterment, and becoming an even more complete version of you.

Suddenly, you understand. You realize that the very meaning of this place is moving up into higher and higher floors of the building. Once you recognize the pattern, you can see people, men and women of different appearances, professions and ages, moving toward different floors of this building. Now, you start seeing the incredibly busy corridors leading to staircases. From the ground floor, you can see that people on the higher floors seem happier than those on the ground floor; they seem to have a different kind of energy. After watching for a while, you begin to understand that moving up higher does not mean only having more money and material opulence. Slowly, it becomes more clear to you that moving higher actually means becoming more—you start understanding that having more is equal to 'being more'. Having more involves change from within. Everything starts making even more sense now. Obviously, the conditions and quality of life have increased by each floor, so at each higher floor level, a better life is lived out by the stair climbers.

But then you notice one strange thing – the staircases are really crowded! They are jammed with people climbing up, almost stepping on the legs of the person in front of them. You look around and notice the numerous entrances, leading to staircases placed on all sides of this building; at every point, you see a similar situation. You want to move up as well. Finally, you find a staircase that looks a bit better by comparison to the other spots that you have just checked. You start climbing enthusiastically, but it does not take long for difficulties and calamities to appear, one after another. You start to notice more and more disturbing details.

Many people are climbing the stairs in that crowd. Although most of the men and women appear to be intelligent, positive, and self-aware, something does not look right. You decide to investigate, to understand more about that 'not right' sixth sense sending you warning signals.

Observing the interaction, you notice that some people, instead of helping others, do many things (some do everything possible) to make others miserable and slow down their climbing pace. Some people appear to be stuck; as they sit on the sides of the staircases, they are often stomped on by the fast-moving crowds, who climb over those seated as if they do not see people sitting down, right in front of them.

From close up, practically every person around this busy place look really unhappy but, for some reason, everyone appears to accept that climbing their staircase as the ultimate reality or 'all there is'. All manner of different traps have been positioned all over the stairs and between the floors; most of them are hidden and very difficult to see.

Another detail that you notice is even worse: a person cannot just sit and rest on the staircase. As soon as one decides to rest for more than a few minutes, gravitation pulls that person down with incredible force, somewhere down toward the ground floor level, but most often to the infamous underground floors.

While moving along, you overhear some horrible stories about what happens in the underground floors of the building: people are forced to work at jobs they hate. They have to work 10 to 12 hours a day or even longer, travel a long way to their jobs and back, just to spend a really short time with their loved ones. Most underground workers suffer from a variety of health conditions and anxieties; they can never feel secure or get any real rest and relaxation. Any earnings made on those underground floors will be taken by debt collectors who rule and control the underground levels.

You begin to hear frightened whispers about a really scary topic: it's quite easy to slip and fall to the underground levels. Some people fall and disappear for a long time, and many never come back...all due to minor mistakes. People seem to be eternally trapped there; many are simply unable to escape the "rat race" of the underground levels.

You now realize that the staircase-climbers are overflowing with tears, sweat, unnecessary suffering, and pain. You don't like what you see, so you start searching, looking for a better way. From within, you simply feel *there <u>must be a better way</u>!* You hope that you can find that way. You continue to search for clues, hoping to see anyone who reaches the higher floors without participating in this messy, painful, and unpleasant climb.

Soon after, by chance or design, you notice the existence of a massive, intricately carved wooden door, placed right behind the beginning of a staircase. The door is somewhat hidden, but it's also not too difficult to find if you're looking for it. When you look slightly closer, you understand that it is an elevator door. The numbers and the display placed above clearly indicates this door as a way to an elevator from the ground to the top floor. On a walk around the ground floor corridors, you quickly discover that these doors are placed everywhere, in the same location, right around the corner next to each and every staircase around the building. That dark red brown color, and very detailed woodwork on the massive door of mahogany, definitely gives the impression of something even more luxurious and exclusive compared to the luxury one can see in various parts of this building.

Now what now looks really strange to you, and makes you wonder how this can be possible, is an odd occurrence. Despite the fact that these elevator doors are placed at the beginning of each and every staircase (right in front of the noses of everyone moving toward the staircase), very few people notice and try to use this elevator.

THIS IS PROBABLY THE STRANGEST OBSERVATION SO FAR: Since elevators are constructed of strong, nearly unbreakable glass, one can easily see through the walls. Everyone on the ground floor can easily see the passengers in those elevators swooping upward, all the way to the highest floors. Men and women who climb the stairs, even without any crowds or obstacles, or any other staircase calamities, have a much longer way—by at least 100 times—compared to the elevator passengers. Due to the elevators' clear glass doors, that fact is easy to see! Still, most people fail to recognize that.

Compared to the crowd of people climbing the stairs, there are very few elevator passengers. Regardless, those who take the elevator are happy; their faces are beaming with energy and enthusiasm. Anyone can see that, but most people just don't. It's so very strange!"

<<<- END OF INTERACTIVE MEDITATION.

QUESTION: The only condition for using this elevator is to locate it and know what you want to achieve, which floor you want to visit. Obviously, at each higher floor, there is a better lifestyle, level of happiness, and overall sense of material and spiritual satisfaction. If you could choose, which floor would be your choice? Instead of asking the obvious question ("Are you going to choose the staircase or elevator?"), there is a bigger question to ask: "Where are all these people headed?"

I cannot know everything about your situation but I know that you must have a strong desire, a need for something that finally works. The fact that you have read up to this very point tells me that. Also, you are a fair and honest person, not jumping from chapter to chapter in order to quickly jump to the 'really good stuff,' for example. For that reason, and in order to give this method a chance, I want to thank you - and congratulate you!

As I see from numerous examples, sincere seekers always do take an elevator. A person who is sincere enough, will eventually find one. A truly sincere seeker never gives up, which is how they eventually find the best way, something that really can provide a desired change. Climbing the stairs is definitely better when compared to a life in the 'underground levels'; it is also great exercise for burning fat and improving cardiovascular health. However, on a path to financial freedom and the evolution of consciousness, climbing the stairs is surely not a smart move.

Seriously, who wouldn't take the elevator ride and avoid all of the struggle, pain, and risk on the 'do or die' staircase? The methods and approach given in this book, as well as the upcoming books in the series, will provide you with not only a direction to an elevator but also a smooth elevator ride to the highest destination of your choice.

EVER EXPANDING

ON YOUR JOURNEY FROM THE GROUND TO THE TOP FLOOR, YOU CAN CLIMB THE STAIRS OR, IF YOU KNOW HOW, SIMPLY TAKE THE ELEVATOR

At the beginning of my journey, *I did not know* anything about the shortcut; there was no nearby elevator, or at least, nowhere near the area I could see and perceive for a long time. It took me quite a while just to start searching for it. As soon as I understood the significance of the need to switch from the staircase method to something a lot better, it appeared! Once I found an elevator, wow.... *Everything has changed with lightning speed.* Every effort showed results; every internal change I worked on was crowned with external manifestations of success. I started to live again ...

Getting to the REAL shortcut means the elevation to higher vibrations and getting free of blockage after blockage, obstacle after obstacle.

This is most certainly the strongest, most positive experience I had ever lived through. The **best part** about all of this, however, is that the journey *isn't over!* I'm still on that journey that makes me further expand and grow. It has never stopped inspiring and assisting me and it **will never stop** – the only thing that can stop this process is *your own decision*. That is really the best part about the *'Shortcut to Having More'*–it continues to clear all that stops us from moving forward quickly; it expands our inner energy field and consciousness. The process given in this book is a foundation or a complete system that, in reality, makes us expand into an *ever-increasing, improved version* of ourselves. Earning much more is the first thing you will experience but that's only a start. A better quality of life, better relationships, the creation of more wealth, and deeper spiritual connections are part of the process that will gift you with the next level change.

PART I.

STRUGGLING THROUGH A NEW BEGINNING

After losing my business and most of my savings, it took me a few weeks to deal with panic. After that, it took about twice as long to stop whining and move on. I decided to start building my business again, this time on a basis of inner values. The secret of success has a healthy basis –a sound, clear foundation of great importance, right? Yeah, right. If you get to it!

I have tested and tried all sorts of methods; to my knowledge, I have engaged in every single approach, book, audio, or video program of each and every self-development 'guru' that made sense. I have read and experimented, learning and trying to understand it in real-life terms, applying and trying to find out what works. Fellow seeker, you know the drill. In the beginning, you are excited, thrilled, full of hope...but only what happens after that initial honeymoon period gives us real advancement. In my experience, therein lies the exact problem. Some of those things helped, but most of it did NOT. Why? Not because these approaches were wrong or bad, no. I noticed something else that resonated with the person I used to be.

MOST PEOPLE ON THIS PATH JUMP FROM PROGRAM TO PROGRAM, FROM AUTHOR TO AUTHOR, CHANGING SYSTEMS, SIMPLY COLLECTING VIRTUAL DUST ON PILES OF MATERIALS (JUST LIKE I DID) BECAUSE THEY "HAVE TO". WHY? A SIMPLE ANSWER – DESPITE THE EFFORT INVESTED, THEY GOT NONEXISTENT (OR WEAK) RESULTS!

In my experience, most authors, authorities, and gurus want to genuinely help; some are totally convinced they do! All of them seemed to be very helpful in the beginning, but the reality of going through the process was quite different for the end user. Look, I'm not one of those people who only collect programs and books without investing time and effort. On the contrary, I truly have a down-to-earth practical mindset. Like most people, seeking tangible results and practical benefits was (and continues to be) the main purpose. I was always ready to invest time and effort, following exactly what was given, explained, and recommended. For that reason, after spending quite some time in trying my best to do everything right, to reorganize ....to do just about everything as asked or required, I began to realize that the outcome was not heading toward a desired destination, so disappointment appeared on the scene.

DISAPPOINTMENT FEELS REALLY BAD ... YOU FEEL BETRAYED AND FRUSTRATED.

You understand the topic; you feel it, love it, and follow the instructions and teachings. After a while you start getting it...but that's not all. You still sense that something is missing from this situation.

Yes, I know about these frustrations from within. Some of the teachings that I have applied (even quite popular and widely marketed), I can whole-heartedly describe as 'destructive'. Yes, destructive, because the teachers have sold an idea that was nicely shrouded in truth and the longings of the soul; in any real or practical sense, the ideas are just a utopian dream. Some of you have had similar experiences, so we have something in common.

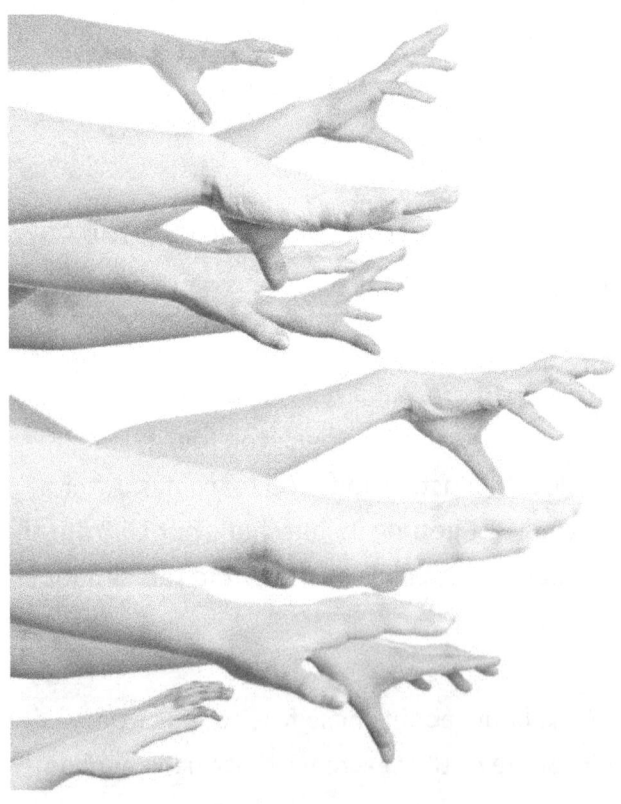

I choose to believe that you are looking to find not only answers, but also practical methods and tools that can actually help you grow, though there is one point I really cannot emphasize enough. From far and wide, we hear that inner growth can ONLY result in the expansion of material prosperity. Most people agree on this. But if that external manifestation DOESN'T appear, if I cannot see and experience it, where is the effectiveness and value of the 'growth'? This is the simple point I am trying to make; all of us want to earn more, achieve more, and have more in DIFFERENT aspects of life, and most of us want that as soon as possible.

As I mentioned before, twenty-two years ago, due to my stupidity in trusting those who were experts at taking everything from me, and without much of a chance to prevent it, I lost nearly all my material possessions: a profitable business, a fully owned house, and most of my savings. As a result, I felt completely lost, ashamed, betrayed, and totally worthless. It took me a while to move out of that miserable condition but I just knew that I must find a solution. I think I always knew that if I really wanted significant change, I would have to change from the inside out.

Over a period of seven or eight years, I was doing these things:

- Spending all my time and money to find out the best way to *get more, become more and be more*.
- Dedicated to all I had been practicing,
- Consistent in my attempts and efforts,
- (Most often) misled and even cheated by different experts and gurus, and
- Despairing and inches away from giving up, several times.

But I had to find a way to continue. Pain and disappointment, interwoven with the hardships of everyday life, wasn't a pleasant place to be. But I had to find a way out, and I did.

'AHA' (Or, There IS an Elevator) Moment

The truth is that I didn't really have an option—I simply had to find the way out. I kept looking for the best way out because I wanted to keep my sanity. I will skip over the details of this really long, painful road. After many disappointments, a long-expected and hoped-for change, or maybe a shift 'back to my roots'—eventually light has started appearing in my approach. I remember the exact moment when I got to this moment of truth – the realization that was practically a precursor for the avalanche of great things that began moving in my direction soon afterward.

In one hard moment of frustration, the old bitterness of a desperate state of mind allowed me to remember one of the most important, basic facts that appear in most philosophical and spiritual books of genuine and original source material. This is the simple fact that we are never alone—each of us is an eternal spiritual entity residing in a material body, but never alone. We all carry in our hearts our 'eternal companion,' our higher self, supersoul, light, spiritual ego, supreme soul, etc. You can use any other designation or identification but the fact remains the same. (For some of you this may sound a little 'off' but I promise that soon, when we start working with methods and techniques, this will become clear and very useful).

As soon as I began listening to my inner voice in a particular way, everything started changing–fast. I regained my ability to recognize things I really needed, and distinguishing people I could trust from those others who should be avoided. It was an incredible experience! It felt just like regaining an old forgotten skill, something that I was never supposed to forget or stop relying on! It has given me the clarity that has changed everything. The process of 'regaining' or 'relearning' is not that difficult; it was in front of my nose all the time. Remember the elevator story from the previous chapter?

THIS ABILITY AND MEANS OF STRENGTH WAS

ALWAYS IN FRONT OF MY NOSE.

However, until I sought a way out using staircase-like methods, made and trapped by material concepts, I couldn't even see the elevator; it was distant and detached from my awareness. In reality, the best solution has been and still is available to anyone.

But is that solution really reachable by anyone? No, not anyone—but it is easily available to anyone who is sincere and ready to explore beyond the (material concepts) box. Many people, assisted by organized marketing teams, try (in lots of ways) to make us think they possess all kinds of powers: mystical, supernatural, psychic, etc. Others insist they possess all-powerful methods leading to pushbutton solutions, ultimate and complete remedies for the vast range of financial and other troubles that any human being can possibly have. We are supposed to believe that their 'gift', system, method, or approach is something extraordinary, something that can help us. For example, many of these people claim that listening to their inner voice is something exclusive, a gift that only the chosen ones can possess. That cannot be further or more removed from the truth!

Even worse are individuals who really are gifted with some amount of additional psychic dose, but are misusing that ability for their own particular selfish reasons. Also, unfortunately, there is a widespread disease—a plague of those who work hard to make us believe they are really genuinely interested to help us (and are able or gifted to do so) while their actual intentions and abilities are nothing but false.

A few more words about the fake 'gurus', psychics, and teachers: Do not think I am closed-minded. I know there are real genuine givers out there, people with pure intentions, real psychic power, and the ability to help others; I also know that those individuals are extremely rare. These unique women and men do not normally market themselves, and are not well known. Even if you managed to meet such a genuine being, he or she won't be able to teach you or transfer their powers unto you. All in all, there is a great deal of garbage out there. Please do not misunderstand the subject we are reviewing with anything coming from the world of make-believe, from La La Land.

SHORTCUT TO HAVING MORE

WHAT WE NEED IS THE ABILITY TO CUT THROUGH THE LAYERS OF THE MIND AND FALSE EGO, TO PROVIDE US ALIGNMENT WITH OUR REAL SELVES, A WAY THAT WILL *ALWAYS* RESULT IN PRACTICAL METHODS OF ALIGNING WITH OUR HIGHER SELF.

By this statement, I do mean always, for everyone, without fail. It may sound more complicated than it really is. The real desire of the spirit-soul in the human body is to be aligned with something we can call 'source energy'. Our relation to the higher spiritual dimension of existence is just like the relation between a drop of the ocean with the Ocean itself, that immensely huge body of water from where the drop originates. That is definitely an environment where the drop really wants to reside and where it feels best. Just like a drop of the ocean, we have our Source. All of us are, by nature, energy transcendental to matter, yet residing and living out this experience in material bodies. Too many people depend on methods that are encapsulated in layers and concepts made of an inferior nature. Any one of these teachings will force one to 'climb the stairs', suffer, and take risks instead of taking the elevator.

How does all of this relate to you? You are the one who knows the best answer to this question. As I see it, there is nothing more relevant and useful for any individual with a desire to grow, expand, become more, and get more out of this experience called Life. The upcoming chapters will provide you with complete insight into a single, powerful method (using multiple techniques) that will help you to remove all obstacles and layers that keep people from having more and becoming more.

PART II.

ORIGINS & BASICS

As you will doubtless agree with me, the greatest difference in our reality is not only about what happens during our 'aha' moments, the difference really happens after those moments of inspiration and enlightenment. Once I reached my 'aha' experience (i.e. I remembered what I was not supposed to forget), everything around me, especially the financial aspect of life, has started to line up in its proper place and direction. Life has started turning into an interesting and better experience. If you remember my previously explained experience of losing practically all of my material possessions, then this statement is enormously positive!

The methods that led me here have started forming into a totally different experience and flow of business. I know and I sense that I am on a good track. This isn't like anything I have tried before. Once I started sharing this approach, I saw the same or an even stronger impact on the lives of those people. Since we are all individuals, certain details of the results may sound or look different, but still (after thousands of clients, friends, and readers) the overall result is the same.

Let me continue to be totally honest in a more detailed way. I believe this will also serve as a word of warning. From the outside, these methods that you will start learning (for clearing unwanted layers around our inner power) may sound "too simple" or may remind you of something you have already read or heard. My warm advice to you, and to anyone else who starts walking that path, is this: "Please do not fall into that trap." Our material ego/inner sabotaging system has often taken this shade; many people simply believe in what they hear from their material mind that resists positive change:

- *It cannot be that simple.*
- *I need something more 'complicated.'*
- *I have already heard about 'this'.*
- *'This' can never work for me.*

Be aware, avoid these traps of false ego, and you will be safe.

So, let's get back on topic. What exactly is the origin of my methods, and what exactly comprises the methods I teach and explain in the *'Shortcut to Having More'*? I have been asked the same questions many times; as I have said already, these exact same methods provide the foundation for my coaching practice. I do have detailed answers to your questions, but I do not want to make this introductory part too long. Hopefully, the following explanation will be satisfactory. These are a few brief, clear answers:

Q1: Are you the creator of these methods, or what are the origins?

In part, the answer is "Yes, I am." However, I can also answer "No, I'm not (the creator)." This is why: the methods that you are learning from me have roots in processes that have been known to mankind for thousands of years. Knowledge derived from ancient disciplines such as Yoga or Qigong are present and have an important role, but so is a modern powerful clearing system like Tapping Into Wealth by Margaret Lynch. I owe her a lot, and I am a certified coach (still in a learning process) through her program. Also, I have been studying many bits of original Sanskrit literature. Vedic wisdom offers many answers, and we can find identical principles in many truly wealthy and realized individuals.

The '*Shortcut to Having More*' is an approach that extracts the essence without any fluff, mystification, or unnecessary theorizing around goals and objectives. Once you learn a bit more about me, you will see how I was forced to find out something direct, efficient, and able to deliver fast results.

*Q2: There are so many books and programs available that deal with similar or identical topics. What are the differences of the '*Shortcut to Having More*' approach? How is this different from other ways of clearing the wealth/abundance blocks?*

Besides the answers I have already given, I can tell you that this approach is a fusion of several extremely potent methods that, when used in the proper order and in a logical way, build on the power of each previous method—and create an incredible chain reaction. This will align your intention and attention; your thoughts, expectations, and conscious actions will grow in such a way that you simply **cannot** stay on the same level. With this process, we simply have to grow and become more. As a natural result, we start earning more money practically at the same moment when the process first takes off! The difference is readily apparent from the reason of its creation–I had no choice but to come up with something that really works. Next to everything else, it doesn't contain a single element that is unimportant or unhelpful for moving quickly from where we are to the place where we want to be in the near future.

Q3: Can you show proof about the efficiency of what you are teaching?

The answer depends on the type of proof you need. Can you judge the taste of honey before opening the jar? Everything that I present, I am applying–and I continue to get fantastic results. Also, it's not only my success and example that counts; you can consider hundreds and thousands of transformed lives as proof positive of this concept. Nearly everyone who has directly applied these methods, or indirectly applied through my books, seminars, and coaching program, has experienced many positive and significant changes in their income and ability to generate more wealth. Those of us who have completed the <u>Tapping Into Wealth</u> program are all changed people, improved versions of ourselves! We have doubled, tripled, or even quadrupled our income levels realistically and within short time periods.

Again, many other changes appear in the reality of people who apply methods presented in the *'Shortcut to Having More'*. Some of the methods are clinically proven for their efficiency to heal a person from really bad conditions such as insomnia, PTSD, and dependency on antidepressants (or other intoxicants). We naturally use the methods to remove those things that impede our progress.

Q4: What is the best way to start, and how I can be sure that I will get results?

How can I be sure that you will apply what you read here? Exactly– I can only be sure when you do it; the results will come after application. I will answer this question by example. Let's say you gave me a jar of first-class forest honey, and let's say I had never tasted it before.

So here we are. I thank you for your nice present, and I hold the jar of dark gold honey in my hands, and I ask you the same question: "What is the best way to taste this honey and how can I be sure that I will like it?" What answer would you give back to me? Most probably, you would say something like this: "Taste and see. Open the jar, taste the honey, and you will see!" It's as simple as that.

MANY PEOPLE FACE THIS PROBLEM –THEY ADMIRE THE GLASS AND THE LOOK OF THE JAR FULL OF FIRST-CLASS HONEY INSTEAD OF OPENING IT AND TASTING THE SWEETNESS OF THE HONEY IN THEIR HANDS.

Hopefully, you will think this is sufficient information and an adequate introduction into what we will begin in the next chapter. What you will probably want to know boils down to one reassuring thing. Individuals who decide to give this practice a chance will be equipped with powerful tools; they will see the result of their internal changes on the external material plane, not long after they start practicing.

These are the methods in the *'Shortcut to Having More'*:

- Simple and easy to understand, learn and apply
- Natural and pleasurable
- Free of religious connotations
- Free of fluff (esoteric, philosophical, and all other kinds of padding)

- **Scientific in nature** [Over 100 clinically proven case studies of the Emotional Freedom Technique, or EFT, show users' great improvement and healing from the most horrible traumatic conditions.]
- **Proven to work and deliver great improvement and transformation**

Based on feedback I get from people in my coaching work, I can see these characteristics are important; I hope they resonate with you as well. While coaching one-on-one, hearing about petitioners' experiences, or reading messages shared by various clients, over and over again I can see how much it means to those applying the *'Shortcut to Having More'* methods, to all of those who give this process a chance. Those who are sincere enough to try these methods have experienced their desired changes, and every person HAS that ability.

An even bigger truth, carried within ourselves, is an urge...a type of uncontrollable strong desire to make that step toward growth and achieving what we were meant to achieve. No one in this world can be happy or peaceful without moving toward the meaning and purpose of their own existence in this material reality. This is a really critical part of our understanding: *having more is your birthright!*

Becoming more and having more is definitely a birthright to each and every one of us. We are all sons and daughters of the richest and most powerful entity in this universe, so where can there be any place for scarcity and fear? Why should any doubt the abundant and ever-increasing nature of this universe? Personally, I'm quite sure that deep within your heart, 'something' tells you this exact same thing.

WE ALL HAVE THAT CONNECTION WITHIN US.

This 'something' is not the voice of our inner critic, not the voice of the grinding or disturbed parts of our mind. This inner voice that I speak about is that inner call, that inner feeling that is continually guiding and directing us, always protecting us, that doesn't allow us to fall or fail; when we suffer a setback, it help us stand back and learn from the experience. All of that and a lot more happens, if we listen!

ONE but DIFFERENT

Without going deeper into philosophy, a few concepts (if we can agree on them) will increase our ability to move forward and faster toward receiving all of the benefits provided by the *'Shortcut to Having More'* process. Regardless of what you do or don't believe, these simple few lines will resonate with most of you. In order to answer this question, we should first agree about the answer on the eternal inquiry of mankind: "Who are we?"

Everything around us is energy - moving and inanimate objects as well as all forms of life; concrete, stone, and glass; oceans, forests, rivers, and air; houses and their accessories; computers and our 'dear' mobile phones. Everything is a form of energy. So are human beings. The difference is that, as a living entity in human bodily form, our very nature is entirely different; yet so many do not seem to understand and use the advantages given in the human form of life.

What are the advantages? In addition to our basic instincts and urges—eating, sleeping, mating, and defending ourselves—we all possess free will and the ability to connect with a source of energy, with the "Cause of all causes". Dogs and cats, cucumbers and apples, and any other living being that resides within one of hundreds of thousands of carbon-based life forms simply cannot sit down, read, study, meditate, or think about these questions. They are obliged to care for their basic needs (eating, sleeping, mating, and defending) and nothing else. A person gifted with a human body has not only the ability but also an urge from inside the heart to learn more, become more, have more, and to achieve. That is the difference between a spiritual soul in a human body and a spiritual soul, a living entity that resides in any other type of body on this material plane.

This spiritual entity, this individual soul, is abundant; it's full of eternity, bliss, and knowledge. It is within our deepest core of existence. We are souls– we are living entities with spiritual qualities. We are spiritual sparks that reside in material bodies. By mistake and the profound influence of an eager false ego, we are identified with our material bodies and minds.

WE DO NOT 'HAVE' A SOUL - **WE ARE** the SOUL.

We *do* have a material body and mind, these complex and sophisticated tools we use to create and live out our experiences in this material reality. The real inner nature of each and every living being is spiritual. Problems arise when we, as spiritual entities, misidentify this material reality to be our shelter, real nature, and source of pleasure. Please don't be alarmed; I'm not going to start any kind of 'preaching'. I'm trying to share a basic, yet very essential point that many of us miss entirely–this very point, if missed, stops people from becoming more and achieving more in nearly all aspects of life. Even if you choose to believe that you are this material body or this material mind, that will change nothing. Your beliefs, religion, political orientation, sex, age, skin color and any other material designation will not change the fact that matter and spirit are simultaneously one and different. Yes, in a real sense of the word, one and different within the same time frame. As I have promised, I won't make this book anything near to a philosophical elaboration, so for that reason, this is the shortest explanation I can devise:

CHARACTERISTICS OF ANYTHING MATERIAL: This is a created being that grows or expands, and maintains its size and strength for a time; it grows old or deteriorates, until finally, it dies. Once without living force it becomes a form of dead matter, such as a piece of meat or a lump of any other material element.

CHARACTERISTICS OF SPIRITUAL ENERGY: It is never created; it never grows old or dies. It is eternal, continually existing, and always present. It is full of knowledge and bliss. It is superior to matter; it moves and makes matter to grow, change forms, and expand.

So, if we agree on these completely opposite qualities of matter and spirit, how we can speak about 'oneness' and why is that important? All energies, regardless of their material or spiritual nature, all come from the same source. The source energy is the same and is above this material plane of existence. For that reason, because matter and spirit share the source, we can consider them as 'one'. However, that does not change the fact of matter's inferiority to spiritual energy. Why is this important?

ABOVE the MIND

It is a very important concept because people who primarily identify with their material bodies and minds are not able to move toward their goals in a way that will be most beneficial. One cannot be really successful without at least a basic understanding of these facts. Another question can be used to illustrate this exact point: "Which is more important, a car or the driver of the car?" A car cannot move without a driver, any more than a driver can move without using the vehicle. It is important to take good care of the engine, gearbox, or external appearance of a vehicle but that will not be enough to win races; the driver must be in good shape and maintained well in the first place.

Everyone who desires to become really successful, to grow toward a bigger income and success level, must understand that both body and mind are important. We have to take good care of both body and mind, but if we do not understand the relationship between body, mind, and soul, then it will be difficult to advance quickly. Yes, there are people who have a lot of money and can point toward a lot of material success, but they did not accept or even know about these principles; we must acknowledge that. The main point here is that once you start scratching a little bit below the very polished and attractive surface, you will easily be able to understand, see, and feel (and often be very surprised at) how much fear, anxiety, shame, stress, and negativity is present in the life of a person who depends solely on material concepts. That is a huge difference between those focused solely on material causes, and those who have a deeper understanding.

When we speak about becoming more and having more, we simply do not think about having more negativity, more stress, more anxiety, and more fear. Unfortunately, those who decide and choose to ignore spiritual principles, individuals who do not want to live according to them, those men and women are definitely living lives swimming in those unwanted and often obnoxious conditions. Nobody wants to live in fear; no one truly enjoys high levels of anxiety and stress. You cannot become free of those bonds if you are living out a program constructed purely out of material concepts; this world offers plenty of proof of that bondage. Look around and you can find plenty of examples.

"Mind over matter" is a well-known proverb. However, it is important to understand that spiritual force (the very nature of what we actually are) is superior to any body, matter, and mind. Growth toward spiritual principles is available for each and every one of us, regardless of whether or not we understand these concepts. For that reason, anything that blocks and slows down our path to abundance (being filled with knowledge, joy, and eternity) deserves our attention; we simply have to find a way to remove it. We can either admit this to ourselves or not, but this is <u>the very intention</u> that moves us all; searching for effective ways to clear up anything that keeps us from expansion and advancement, from moving as a living being into higher frequencies and a better life, searching for a better tomorrow. However, an additional problem arises when we cannot see the original problem clearly. If we have no idea what is stopping us and how we are being stopped, naturally we cannot do much in order to overcome that issue.

Even though these last two paragraphs may sound a little philosophical, I will repeat that this understanding is **essential** to ensure swift results. Everything is energy, but not all energy carries the results or experiences that you want for yourself. For this reason, we have to differentiate between the material aspect of the world around us and the spiritual element that we all carry within us.

FREE WILL

Once we start to think about and explore the reasons and causes of our obstacles to earning more money and achieving more, we will encounter several schools of thought that could be boiled down to two types of approaches. Practically speaking, both are partially wrong. Let me explain again without going into a deeper philosophical debate. In these schools of thought are people who claim: *'You are the creator, you have all control, you are creating your own destiny. Everything that you imagine, you can create; you can become anything and everything - there are no limits.'*

Others, on other hand, claim this: *'Everything in this life is already predetermined: our moment of birth, the position of the stars, karma, etc. Destiny has strictly and firmly mapped out our lives. There is no choice; there are only predetermined reactions based on your past decisions (past lives)'*.

From most places, explanations tend to incline toward one of these versions - if not completely colored one way, each explanation is shaded in some significant percentage. What people do not know about is one very important element - this *something* is the only thing that human beings really possess. If 'they' decide to take away everything from us, whatever they do, it is impossible to take away from us that one 'thing', provided we do not willingly surrender or willingly participate in giving away this precious gift. FREEDOM is respected and desired because of this same 'thing'—our freedom of choice.

A FREE WILL, AN ABILITY TO MAKE CHOICES AND DECIDE WHERE NEXT WE WANT TO MOVE/WHAT NEXT WE WANT TO DO, IS ALWAYS PRESENT, IMPORTANT, AND AVAILABLE ETERNALLY TO ALL OF US.

What we are doing is directly responsible for the types of reactions and results we will get in the future. This is the real question: "How are we using it?" What do we do with our ability to choose? What are we thinking about or focusing on?

Basically, this misconception is about the Law of Karma being a one-way street. A person strongly influenced by this version of understanding can be seriously hindered from making rapid success, not only in the spiritual realm but in all other aspects of life. No doubt, you know at least one person who walked into this trap and probably got stuck there. These are a few examples of karmic thinking:

- *"Everything is predetermined, so why should I invest any energy, why should I endeavor?"*
- *"It is the higher arrangement of the universe (higher plan, God, destiny etc.) so I cannot do anything about it."*
- *"Everything seems to be against me. I give up."*

These are just few examples. When people get bewildered by these illusory concepts, their lives turn into intense experiences of pain and suffering. Basically, they give up because they missed out on understanding that *one thing* that could help. The Law of Karma, destiny, or whatever else you want to call it, is not a one-way street. In terms of time, it's at least a two-way street. What exactly do I mean by that?

Since we have free will, we never really lose our ability to decide what we will focus on and do. Yes, we do carry our conditioning from the past (lives);

all of us have different characteristics, capacity, talents, etc. Just as each one of us does not desire identical things, as our goals are all different in some way, so is our ability to achieve those things. Our current problem is that people are controlled and practically brainwashed by mass media; our Internet conditioning is filled with the aggressive promotion of ultra-high levels of consumerism. A person who has been "desire-damaged" (this phrase illustrates much better what actually happens to those who surrender to that powerful influence of media and advertisements washing around us) becomes identified with ideals that are heavily promoted and aggressively advertised. These are some examples:

- I have to earn XYZ amount of money.
- I have to look like this or that model/celebrity/actor etc.
- I have to drive this brand of car.
- I have to do, have, show _____ or else.
- IF I DON'T (have, do, own) _____ then I'm a failure/I won't be happy/I can't be beautiful/I can't look and/or feel successful, etc.

NEWSFLASH: This kind of thinking is all rubbish! This programmed thought pattern kills your growth.

Once we become aware of our real nature, as soon as we manage to cut through the layers covering who you really are, everything changes.

PEELING THE ONION

Before we move on to design your *Personal Wealth Blueprint* and explain other methods, there are just a few more layers to unravel. When we speak about a solution, we must know and identify the <u>root of the problem</u>. Most of those inner obstacles on our path to having more, earning more and being more, these were inherited in our childhood, usually between the ages of 2 to 7. At that age of absorption, our consciousness is extremely vulnerable, reflecting and emulating all that was perceived, heard, or seen. That turns into a foundation of beliefs and programmed perceptions about ourselves, others, and life. We accept other people's beliefs that make us think in certain ways and certain patterns. (Many use this example of peeling an onion, but I love the way it really helps us to understand the real nature of the problem, so we can achieve our goals faster.)

Energy around us consists of many layers. When exposed to so many factors, impressions, beliefs, realizations, and thoughts in our early childhood, the layers of our mind become imprinted with impressions that we absorb. Any potential increase in our ability to earn more and prosper in all aspects of life is unconsciously blocked by negative emotions we managed to absorb as children – emotions and impressions of shame, guilt, fear, frustration, apathy, and so many more. These are blocks to our wellbeing and abundance that directly affect all aspects of a relationship between ourselves and money. Those experiences don't happen just once or a few times. Many times, young children are faced with these (positive or negative) impressions during those few years at we are most open and vulnerable state. For that reason, there are several layers of the imprints and reactions to everything that we accept at that age.

These obstacles are also present in several layers and have to be dealt with good processes of detection and removal. Yes, most of us inherited a lot of unwanted imprints from parents, caretakers, or anyone else around us. Subconscious barriers on your path to *Having More* are rooted in you silently and sneakily, behind the scenes, from many sources: society, family, religion, etc. And they constantly manage to destroy your aspiration to move forward with success. Just like an onion, you have to start from the beginning and continue until you get to the 'best version' of the onion without a single unwanted layer. [Perhaps Abraham Maslow is a reliable source for the definition of a self-actualized person, who has reached the pinnacle of achievement and potential; other well-known examples of those who reached the core of their personal onion might be Abraham Lincoln and Albert Einstein.]

This is the basic idea - all blocks to wealth and prosperity are responsible for a negative or positive impact on our entire lives. Soon, you will have everything you need, piece by piece, to differentiate unwanted elements from those that are good, those that should remain as an important part of your system. It is beneficial to understand the necessity of identifying obstacles to prosperity and wealth. I have met thousands of people held in place and blocked because of various types of barriers in their subconscious mind. The majority had a great number of difficulties because they weren't able to successfully and precisely identify what was stopping them. Naturally, if we cannot identify what slows us down, there is no way we can deal with it and remove it.

THE ACTUAL REASON THAT MAKES US EARN, HAVE, SPEND, AND OWE A CERTAIN AMOUNT OF MONEY IS STORED WITHIN OUR INTERNAL WIRING TOWARD MONEY, WEALTH AND PROSPERITY.

This reason relates to your thoughts, ideas, and beliefs in relation to these areas: cash, money, income, wealth, rich people, and luxury. All of the energy imprints and frequencies received in your life have a certain result in the current quality and frequency of your thoughts, ideas, opinions, and beliefs in making certain decisions. All of these 'programs' <u>force us to take wrong choices</u> and make decisions that are not really best for us.

Tragically, this happens on a daily basis, regardless of the fact that we are conscious or unconscious about it. Yes, my use of the word "force" is intentional. If we do not have a way to detect and deal with our programming, then we will be *unwillingly* and *unconsciously* forced into an auto-response reaction. That of type of response turns into behavioral thinking patterns which more or less turns into a domino effect, a chain of reactions based on the previously formed reaction, and….well, you get the picture. It creates each and every feature, situation, and condition that makes up our current reality. As we can see by this example, ignorance is NOT a blessing. Awareness, on the other hand, is a blessing. Awareness carries an important reminder–knowledge and a clear understanding of why it is not beneficial to slam the door in front of things that bring us closer to growth and prosperity.

PART III.

THE TRUTH ABOUT MONEY

This very topic can be elaborated in a very detailed way; the root of the topic, of course, needs a separate book. First of all, we have to understand the nature of money in the same way. Did you ever think about the essence of money, other than as green paper printed by a government, or as a means of monetary exchange?

While thinking deeper about this topic, many of you may recall different levels of understanding in relation to finance, financial markets, Federal Reserve, conspiracy theories, and any other images dredged up by your mind. That is a very natural response because money in itself <u>appears</u> to be an extremely complex thing. Actually, it can be, but only if we do these two things:

a) Look at it from a plainly material point of view; and

b) Allow ourselves to 'buy into' a material understanding and widely-marketed ideas about money.

Hundreds and thousands of books, case studies, and opinions are offered almost daily about this subject–the true nature of money. But what is actually important for us? Out of that vast body of knowledge, what exactly will *serve our purpose* and help us clear up *everything* that stands in our way of making more money, keeping more money, and (most importantly) doing something that we really enjoy? I believe that these few conclusions below will serve and help you, even if you decide not to put into practice the methods described in this book.

- Money is energy.
- Money is a vessel of value exchange.
- Tune up your vibration and your wealth capacity will change– instantly.

- Detect and delete your blocks so that money will start flowing towards you.
- Freedom from obstacles will show you how to provide even more value to your customers by doing something that you love and enjoy, that brings in even more money.

Most men and women who seek real answers know these principles; most likely, you have found yourself dwelling on them every now and then. When we take the time to enter a little deeper into the meaning behind those principles, we will connect the dots and move much faster toward our goals. Since money is energy and a vessel of value exchange, it is constantly changing and is free to flow wherever conditions are favorable. In simplified terms, once we create conditions for money to flow within ourselves, wealth and money will love us more, visit us more often, and stay with us a lot longer.

Let me share with you a few thoughts as a conclusion. Read and decide for yourself if money and wealth are more spiritual or material in nature.

1)   Money is a tool for getting things done; it is 'conscious' about that fact. Give it a purpose, define exactly what you want to do, and money will 'know' how to come to you.

2)   We do not feel good in the presence of people who do not like us and do not think well about us. We don't like spending time with them at work or visiting in their homes. Those who do not LOVE us, we simply avoid as much as we can. It is exactly the same way with money.

3)   Just like a motivated, spiritually charged person who does things quickly and expertly, money also likes speed...but it dislikes reckless or hasty dealings that diminish the quality of the value shared.

4)   As much as you spend on good causes that really help and create change, that much (or more) money will come to you.

5)   You do not want to appear on the doorstep of a person who has not been expecting you; it's uncomfortable and awkward. Why should money behave differently?

It's interesting, don't you think? The overarching conclusion could be that becoming a truly wealthy, abundant person involves so much more than mere money. Yes, money is an important factor in the process, but answers to 'why' and 'how' seem of larger importance and power than being focused only on a superficial, external understanding of making more money.

COUNTER-INTENTIONS

JUST LIKE A THIEF IN THE PROCESS OF STEALING YOUR VALUABLES, MOVING SILENTLY TO AVOID DETECTION, THESE INFLUENCES LATCH ONTO YOUR SUBCONSCIOUS MIND AND BLOCK DESIRED RESULTS FROM APPEARING IN YOUR REALITY, INHIBITING YOUR ABILITY TO BECOME THE BEST VERSION OF YOURSELF.

You may have already learned something about this term, 'counter-intentions'. Yet to get a deeper understanding and definition of counter-intentions, wouldn't it be best to learn why and how they appear? We have already touched on this topic slightly; however, I would like to share a somewhat deeper type of understanding. Armed with that viewpoint, we will naturally gain an ability to apply upcoming methods with ease; everything presented in the practical part of this book can be approached in a way that will assure great results.

Success, as most of us know, does not depend on a dry theoretical understanding. It's about clarity and direct experience. Knowledge and healthy understanding is about being clear on what actually happens. In other words, it is really insufficient only to realize or identify obstacles to have more arise from the childhood influence of our parents, family, or caretakers. How, exactly?

As a child, didn't you hear your parent's varied complaints about the difficulties of their lives? Did they talk about how 'the government always takes the side of the rich', while the masses were unheeded? Or perhaps you heard your mother, father, or caretakers using lines and conclusions such as these:

"Who do you think I am - Rockefeller???"

"Oh really, do you think that money grows

on trees?"

"That is too expensive. Find something cheaper, something normal."

"Are you crazy? This is not for people like us."

"Play safe, go to school, get a good job...that's how it works."

These are only examples of many similar statements that are definitely not beneficial, especially when the mind of a young person starts to wholly believe in the statement, accepting it as a complete reality without any other options.

With respect to people who grew up in *religious families* or families that are *spiritually* oriented, even if the family did not strictly follow one religion or philosophical teaching, there are still issues–perhaps differently colored. The problems they face were also hidden within the belief systems they grew up with. Starting from the most obvious and widely spread phrase, "the love of money is the root of all evil" (whereas the original phrase states "the **love** of money is the root of **all kinds** of evil"), all the way to a subtler phrase (yet of the same destructive strength) "it is not spiritual to be wealthy," life gets quite complicated when you are under siege from these subconsciously programmed thinking and acting patterns.

Some, or maybe even all, of these statements may sound harmless to you. Not many people take the subject seriously. Most of us, even when we are aware of these phrases at some level, hardly notice the devastating and severe influence they have on our lives and ability to grow and expand. Silently, they sneak into your subconscious mind and create unwanted thought patterns that contain the power to destroy the life and future of a person who is trapped and controlled by them. These days, another approach has gained popularity; it shares the same risky and dangerous nature as the ignorance or total mind control encouraged by these programmed limited beliefs. That popular approach, especially in New Age, esoteric circles, is stealing our ability to dig deep and solve the problem at its root.

It is easy to say and think: "THERE ARE BLOCKS IN MY SUBCONSCIOUS MIND, THERE ARE LIMITING BELIEFS, UNWANTED THOUGHTS AND THOUGHT PATTERNS. I SIMPLY HAVE TO OVERCOME THEM."

Well, that only dimly resembles the actual situation and solution. The problem, however, is hidden in a mindset underlying that one particular word – 'SIMPLY'. If that was *really so simple*, why are there so many people who are stuck, unable to achieve their plans and goals? Why would you read this book in the first place? That's the trick the mind plays and unfortunately, many buy into it. The solution is simple but it's not superficial.

I have been promising you powerful, practical, and crystal-clear ways of detecting and dealing with all these obstacles. You can be certain that is exactly what you will get. In this step, we have to face the fact that understanding the existence of that problem or issue isn't enough. As with awareness, one cannot solve a problem created today by maintaining the same state of mind, habits, thoughts, and behavioral patterns. The *'Shortcut to Having More'* provides a simple (but not superficial) understanding in this theoretical part of the book. Nobody can create real results and derive satisfaction by simply 'knowing' about the problem superficially – we need to really know what exists before we know exactly how to solve it.

> MORE THAN ONE INTENTION IS INFLUENCING AND DIRECTING YOUR LIFE. THEREFORE, YOU GET A MIXED BAG OF RESULTS. THEREFORE, SOMETIMES YOU FEEL LIKE DRIVING WITH THE PARKING BRAKE ON.

Unfortunately, counter-intentions that stop or slow us down don't only relate to our childhood. As life rolls on, the structure and strength of counter-intentions can grow into a large snowball effect; your entire environment will contribute, including rock stars, Hollywood actors and actresses, and other VIP personalities. These affect your life as you unconsciously let these programs into your life, more on top of more. This is because you love them and you want to *be like them*; in the case of your parents and other role models, you want them to love you back. These influences are piling up; if not dealt with, it becomes harder and harder to clear them out.

Having said that, there is always a chance; it is never too late to start. Based on my own and (even more importantly) others' experiences from whom I have learned, it is entirely true that each and every one of us can resonate, vibrate, and attract wealth by clearing all of these programs.

DEVASTATING NATURE OF COUNTER-INTENTIONS

Sometimes I get questions from clients or seminar participants that everyone can relate to, on some level. The question, more or less, sounds like this: *"I don't need more money. I have enough money for comforts, and I live the life I want to live. Why should I care about all these counter-intentions, limiting beliefs, inner blockages to wealth and abundance, or any of those things?"*

Good question! Without going into a discussion about "how much money is enough" and the real reasons that makes someone ask this question, in answer to these types of enquiries or doubts, I use the example of driving a car at full speed with the parking brake on. You can drive a Lamborghini Diablo, a BMW 760i Alpina BiTurbo, a Prius, or a crappy Yugo, but if the parking brake is left on, you will experience the same type of problem every time. It will sound and act differently, depending on the car, but its essential nature and functionality will be very similar. To make a long story short, if one understands the real nature of money and wealth, one gets a clear answer and can avoid the position of asking this question at all. Counter-intentions reach down deep, limiting and compressing not only our ability to earn more, but to have more and become more.

Keep in mind the fact that almost all of our counter-intentions and blocks were absorbed at some point in our lives between the ages of 2 to 7. Many other serious researchers agree about this issue. Many of my certified colleagues and coaches (who use the methods of Tapping Into Wealth, NLP, and Law of Attraction) have confirmed my experience; many of our clients are simply unable to detect these blocks even after 20 years of effort. That is not the only issue, but it is considered as one of the main reasons; simply said, it's very unlikely to find the root of the block itself, after it has been imprinted on us sometime between the ages of 2 and 7.

We already reviewed the characteristics of the inner obstacles, but now let's review them from the eyes of a child, from the perspective of our own eyes when we were small children. After birth, we find ourselves in an entirely new environment; we are totally dependent on the care, attention, and love that we receive. As soon as our senses start gaining in power and functionality, we basically start to mimic all that we see around us. From our surroundings, we understand very soon what feels good and from where goodies come. We quickly learn how to attract more attention, love, and care; as a result, people around you will help you get everything that you need.

That was how we learned to be like others. In the beginning, this process began with our mothers and fathers who loved us, helped us, fed us, and cared for us, so we began to duplicate our whole environment. Unfortunately, very often those around us at an early age didn't have an excellent relationship with wealth and money. That early, mixed imprint of negative energy and attitudes, every spoken statement and every other type of behavior in relation to money and wealth, left different types of limitations and scars on our subconscious minds. Unwillingly we start to mimic these patterns, the same as we have learned to mimic everything else in order to get love and attention.

To further help you closely understand the type of devastation and powerful influence of these counter-intentions, hidden within the subconscious mind of each and every man or woman on earth, I can give one example of a widely spread counter-intention. In my opinion and experience, this block on the path to wealth and abundance <u>must</u> be cleared. This counter-intention is born from the belief that, in order to become successful and wealthy, "We must work hard." It is forced upon the great majority of the population, inherited over and over again throughout generations.

These days, it has become a lot easier to understand and apply change to this paradigm that practically nails individuals to a miserable and painful lifestyle. Just look around and think about your immediate family members, your grandparents, and friends who are suffering from this understanding and belief. They have worked (and continue to work) very hard for their money; sometimes, unfortunately, they exchange their entire lifetime for a very small amount of money. When you compare their lives with the lifestyle of someone who is truly wealthy and financially free, often you can see a huge difference based on this false belief. If we believe we must work very hard in order to earn a small amount, that is exactly what will happen in our lives.

Many people don't even think about changing this idea. The reality is that today, by applying a few different principles, you can start to replace that counter-intention with new ideas and get surprisingly good results in a short amount of time. Just like every other recommendation in this book, I won't offer you the typical worn-out advice to say this type of mantra: "Start believing that money comes easily" or "Every day, in every way, I am doing better and better," or anything like that. When you really learn about the life and the habits of truly wealthy and abundant personalities, you will notice something that you have definitely thought about. All of them achieved their incredible success based on an idea, concept, or activity that they were entirely passionate about. They are (or have been) embodying that idea, concept, service, or activity that served as an earnings channel for millions of dollars, euros, or British pounds.

Instead of thinking, "We have to work hard," they became living examples of the idea that you can get paid for being yourself. As soon as a person changes this part of her belief system, everything outside of her changes or alters in order to serve and fulfill that new belief. I have been playing with this idea without anything really changing, before I started really love it; as soon as I accepted it with all my heart, everything changed in my life. Instead of struggling and working hard, I grew into a person who loves and adores his job. When you really love something, you are entirely willing to go for it without it feeling like a hard thing to do.

Since that switch, many great things have come to me. I have created and shared great value with hundreds, thousands, and even tens of thousands of nice, positive, honest, business-minded individuals who were somewhat stuck and needed an additional boost on the path of growth. That was naturally followed with incredible financial rewards for them and for me. That is the power of changing counter-intentions.

EVERYTHING CHANGED WHEN I DECIDED TO BE PAID SIMPLY FOR BEING ME.

Again, it is not that hard to replace your old

negative programs and counter-intentions. Unfortunately, this is not something you can do alone, without a method that works. That is one quite popular 'loop' without either an exit or solution; many people think they can deal with all of their counter-intentions and obstacles on their own. Of course, you can work hard on a particular problem, belief or idea, but without raising your vibration, without elevating your ability and understanding, you will still be blocked; you will not really be successful.

If we don't use a really powerful approach or method, we simply can't get that necessary energy to uproot those deeply rooted blockages that all of us retain to a certain degree. You feel stuck; your plans and objectives are often defeated by inner, counter-programs that often pull you back. That is exactly why it is so important to clear counter-intentions and replace them with new ones. Without doing that, you will keep regressing into a non-abundant frequency and loophole of existence. To grow, you simply *need* to clear your (conscious and subconscious) mind from all blocks and obstacles to raise your energy frequency to where it must be.

Limiting beliefs and counter-intentions, if they

are not cleared out of our systems, will create a measurably painful life and a sure path of stagnation and deterioration. As soon as one starts to walk this path of change, his or her energetic field starts to transform into something entirely different; with the right frequency, the change will remain with you forever. As soon as you start going in this direction, circumstances and new people will appear in your reality in order to help you. I will do my best to provide you with all of the knowledge and tools you need.

I am sure you will build significant results for yourself based on the *'Shortcut to Having More'* when you get into a routine of using these methods. Having said that, we will start with the practical methods and processes.

Part IV.

METHOD EXPLAINED

CONNECTING TO THE SOURCE

IMPORTANT NOTE: *If you are serious about the process, I'm providing you with a complete package and ongoing support; for those who would like assurance, you **will** be getting everything on time. To reach maximum effectiveness, you will need our tools, handouts, videos, and MP3 recordings; please request them from* [this link](#)*, https://events.genndi.com/register/169105139238463108/25333aea67. (Be sure that we will not misuse your email address in any way, shape, or form). Once we receive your best email address, you will be sent an email to confirm your subscription. If you do not see it in one hour after you subscribe, please check your spam folder and all inboxes. Very soon after confirming your subscription, you will receive the first email with support materials related to the first process, as* *described in this chapter. Within seven days after the first email, you will receive a second email with tools and complete support related to the second part of this practice.*

This is an introductory exercise of connecting to our source energy; it is used before applying any other techniques and methods that you will learn. In fact, you can even apply this method in your morning ritual to gain a lot more energy and focus. For our purposes, your morning ritual would include anything you do regularly in the morning: before jogging, after a shower, morning coffee, meditation, visualization, goal-setting, etc. Anything you do will result in better quality.

To be clear, connecting to the source energy is a method of conscious and natural alignment with the pulse and energy of the universe. Everything around us is energy, our bodies and minds are made of energy, but each and every form of energy has its source. You can call it 'source energy' or you can use any other name; that is not important here. There is a source and there is a Source of all sources as well.

Our lifestyles have encouraged us to neglect

alignment to this source energy, a form of energy that is constantly present, freely available, and always ready to help us; this source energy will support and drive us toward our real nature and to the achievement of our goals. The fact is that we are always in connection, but not always in conscious alignment, with the source energy. Regardless of any belief system or religious background, you can relate to existence of a dimension that is *by nature* above our plane of existence. Their energy has its source and we can connect to this source energy in a conscious way; after a few days or weeks of practice, you won't need the help of this book or MP3 recording anymore. (Again, if you didn't yet send in a request, you can request this and other support materials from the link provided here, *https://events.genndi.com/register/169105139238463108/25333aea67*)

In the beginning, I would recommend that you use the book or recording in order to facilitate and speed up the learning process. What you will notice (and what really amazes me) is the speed at which people learn this process. Of course, you need to take some time and effort to learn, but it really goes faster you can imagine now. Why? Because this is nothing new for a human being. It is actually a re-learning process, more like remembering something that is already in us but forgotten for a while ... based on that idea, it feels natural. After the initial learning phase, using this process, you will be able to connect and, soon after, *stay* connected to the source energy—practically whenever you wish. The amount of 'heart' you bring to this simple practice will push it to quickly become an automated and perfectly realized action.

In fact, various ancient cultures, mystical practices, methods of self-realization, and other transformational practices have used this method in one way or another. We are presenting it to you in a very direct and simplified way that everyone can learn and use with success.

Two Source Energy Centers

We will reach out and connect to the *two source energy centers*; one is located above us and one is located below us. In these areas, ethereal and material dimensions are closely interrelated—dimensions where it is easy to connect with the source energy. Of course, energy is omnipresent; it exists everywhere in its pure and most complete form. Call it Qi (Chi), Prana, Ki, Light, Universal Energy, God's Energy or by any other name you want; the fact is we are dealing with one and the same energy.

Instead of spending a good part (or even the whole) of your life to master a method of connecting to the source energy, now you can use this short and clear method that will actually provide you with everything you need in order to accelerate your *'Shortcut to Having More'* results. Naturally, there is a lot more to it, but this intellectually basic level is (believe it or not) more than enough; it is extraordinarily effective and beneficial to everyone who takes it seriously. Regardless of what you believe or do not believe, this force drives all living entities in this universe, and is freely present all around us. However, it doesn't do us many favors if we do not know how to align to it. In this modern age, the majority of us have become distant to almost anything and everything that is natural; these types of skills, like aligning to source energy, have been long forgotten by many.

The center ABOVE

First, the source energy center that you will connect to is located approximately 300 feet above us (regardless of your location, from sea level on up). This sphere's location is relevant to everyone as long as you are somewhere on planet Earth. From that sphere, we can connect to pure source energy much easier; one starts to feel it very fast, and very often after only 10 to 15 practice sessions. If you have prayed or meditated before at an intense level, you will be able to remember this feeling, a warm and energized vibration of being connected; it always comes naturally. If you are visual and it helps you to imagine and use images, you can visualize this sphere as an ocean of golden, liquid light. Many people with a developed inner (subtle) sense describe this area that wraps around our planet.

\\\\\\\\\\\

The center BELOW

The second source energy center is located in the center of our planet Earth. In a similar fashion to the previous explanation, you do not need any instruments or artificial ways of aligning your energy with the source energy that is present in the center of mother Earth. This planet has supported and tolerated humankind for a long time now; it does suffer and has been scarred by our fellow humans in so many ways. However, it continues to provide us with everything we need for life and existence. One essential and (literally) most important element for our survival is this very same source energy that we are working with above. Naturally, this center BELOW us is the opposite polarity of the ABOVE energy center; similarly, it is quite easy to feel it, approach it, and establish contact with it.

Once you start with that part of the exercise, you will simply project your energy toward this ocean of energy that sustains our planet and life on our planet, and you will capitalize on its power to automatically connect with the ABOVE center. Once you consciously expand your energy up and below, you will be able to feel its strength. As soon as your energy reaches to it, you will feel as it is catapulted with force (while simultaneously of a caring, gentle, and almost elegant nature) right up to your heart. People who develop their inner senses, who see energy, often describe this zone as an ocean of bright lights that carry a bluish glow. If it helps you to visualize, feel free to use that image if it suits you.

A few things before you start:

Arrange a peaceful space (as peaceful as it can be) without disturbance for the next 5 or 10 minutes. It would be helpful to switch off your mobile phone, notifications from Facebook, Skype, Instagram, etc. If you're using the provided MP3 recording, you'll get the best results by using headphones.

When you first start learning, arrange yourself in a sitting or standing position. Later on, we can do this while lying down. However, it is not recommended to do that in the learning phase, specifically to avoid slips and falls.

If you're sitting, it's best to choose a surface that is not too soft, in order to keep your back fairly straight. Sit comfortably, with both feet firmly touching the ground. Relax as much as you can and breathe naturally. Do not cross your legs and arms if possible. Breathe in and out, two or three times, before the start of the exercise.

GUIDED EXERCISE - CONNECTING TO THE SOURCE ENERGY

Look up or extend your intention above, lifting up your energy to about 300 feet above your head, all the way up to the ABOVE center; this is a place where you can feel, sense, or see the source energy. Simply reach out to this place, to the dimension where the source energy is freely available. Take a deep breath and do not worry about how the whole process will go, because no matter how this happens, you will be fine. This ocean of golden source energy is the space or region from where you take your life energy; it is a place where all living entities in this universe get their power to move, create, and grow. Once your attention reaches this place, connect to it and allow the source energy to flow downwards. You can feel or visualize a strong beam of golden energy flowing down and reaching the top of your head. Now, you can ask this golden light to clean all of the negative energies and patterns in you and around you. Let this golden light go further down, and reach your eyes, removing all negative programs and beliefs you have ever accepted.

Allow this golden liquid energy to move further down and reach your throat, removing all blocks that do not allow you to create your future. Then, let this light penetrate your heart area and clean you from all accumulated anger, fear, and frustration that weakens you. Bring this molten golden light toward your torso and stomach area, entirely deleting energy related to giving up, as well as feelings of being stuck and powerless.

Then go further down, bringing energy to your hips and root, where this cleansing power melts away all self-doubt and blocks to growth. Let the light travel down your legs and once it reaches your feet, let it ground you with absolutely new and inspiring energy. You are now connected to the center Above and this cleansing energy is flowing from the top of your head, all the way down to your feet.

From there, project the energy downward, right toward the center of the earth. The energy of Earth is felt as a mother's love; it provides wonderful feelings of safety and security, peace and happiness. When golden energy reaches the center of the source energy that beams from the center of the planet, it becomes strongly catapulted back upward and toward your feet, hips, and stomach, and finally it reaches back to your heart area. When these two energies meet, your heart area, body and mind, is filled with an abundant energy of creation.

Take a deep breath ... you are connected to the source. You feel safe and secure. You feel this connection with the source energy from above and below. Feel the energy flow from both directions. Now, you are full of the energy of creation, abundance, safety, and security. You are completely soaked in powerful source energy and your heart area now becomes a center where these energies meet.

Now, from your heart, start expanding this energy out, beyond your body. It is easy to do; just ask it to expand and it will happen. Expand your energy in a radius of 12 inches (one foot) around your body. Continue and expand your energy further out, reaching out to a radius of to 5 to 10 feet around you. Fill the room you're in with energy and continue beyond that. Fill the building where you are with energy and expand beyond that. Go further and expand it as far as you can. Reach out to the borders of your city, region, and country.

You are now connected with limitless source energy that can be expanded from your heart all the way around the globe, then all the way around the entire universe. Now, you are connected with the source of all wealth, knowledge, abundance, and creation - and this most powerful creative source energy is streaming through you. Unlimited possibilities are being created for you right now. All parts of your body and mind are healing and becoming stronger. You are now becoming the best version of yourself. You are taking a shortcut to

Having More.

This is the end of the Connecting to the Source Energy exercise. If you are ready to practice it regularly for at least 21 days in a row, you can be sure that it will not only become a powerful, pleasing experience but also it will happen more and more by default, so much so that you will find your way to using it in practically any life situation. To be connected with the source energy is something you can (and should) use for your own benefit. It will bring abundance, not only of financial growth but also improvement in other aspects of life (health, physical, mental, and emotional).

HOMEWORK:

Again, once you start practicing, you will probably need help. You can use the Connecting to the Source Energy MP3 or video; if you think you don't need it, you can do this exercise by help of the text above. You can practice this at any time of day; however, the best time for it is early morning, before the sunrise. Gradually, you will find the process becoming natural and easy as time passes, depending on the amount of practicing and focus that you invest in this exercise. After a short while, you will notice that you do not need the help of the recorded MP3-guided meditation, video, or even the text. As with anything else in life, "practice makes the master." In any case, please do this exercise for the next seven days, at least once a day, before moving to the next part of this book. By all means, you can certainly read it, but please be patient. Do not begin applying the next method until you get tuned into Connecting to the Source Energy practice. *It is really important* and will help you derive much more from the upcoming parts of the "Shortcut to Having More" system.

PS: This following short piece of advice is for the restless readers who are feeling the urge to jump right to the next part without practicing this method for at least five to seven days, once or (much better) twice per day. I admire everyone who is eager and ready to invest time and energy in order to grow faster; however, I feel that a strong word of advice is necessary for you to hear. If you jump-start the process by working with the next part of our method before getting accustomed to Connecting to the Source Energy, the time needed to materialize results (that we would really like to see you achieve) will be unnecessarily prolonged. I am quite sure that you don't want that to happen. There are enough things slowing you down anyway, so for that reason, please stick to the plan. After getting accustomed to Connecting to the Source Energy, at least once a day for the next seven days, then you can safely move to the next part.

YOUR PERSONAL WEALTH BLUEPRINT

Introduction

By now, I hope you are familiar with the Connecting to The Source Energy practice. Again, that will multiply your results many times over. For many of you, this will create all of the necessary conditions for our new start. Over my years of working on my own issues and then becoming a coach, it became very clear to me that one of the biggest things we need to get very specific about (when pursuing great and measurable outcomes of transformational work) related to money and wealth. Many people are generalists – they do general work around abundance and the Law of Attraction, without getting specific. I learned that it's one of the biggest problems that causes people a lot of pain, suffering, and disempowerment. It breaks up families and individuals' careers, stopping people from doing what they love–yet it's not addressed in a very specific way.

This exercise is based on Margaret Lynch's approach and teaching; it is definitely one of the most complete and powerful clearing systems available today. As a certified 'Tapping into Wealth' coach, I have been using her approach to bring light and clarity to very specific blocks, and it has worked wonders with me and my clients. Once we have clarity about the five different forms of money, we can actually start clearing away obstacles with much better results to open possibilities into an entirely different world. It is very difficult to act properly or even have a good plan without having clarity. This is essential because everything with value is born from clarity. Without it, we can't progress, be decisive, or even focus on what we want because we are confused.

Most of us know that inner impediments and barriers are stopping us from earning and keeping more money, but rarely does anyone get specific and clear on the exact types of blocks in our way and how to remove them. Why should you lose time and energy on anyone else's issues but your own? One very important point is a mind-body money connection. All of you know of the 'mind-body connection'—the way our autonomic nervous system transmits and causes change in the body based on what we are thinking about. Images and thoughts in our minds trigger emotions and feelings flowing through the nervous system. In a "mind-body money" connection, as you are about to see, different specific forms or types of money will trigger very specific mind-body reactions, blasting through the nervous system. Those reactions are responsible for all emotions and feelings that are spinning through our heads, causing unconscious self-talk and thinking patterns.

The first phase in this exercise will provide you with amazing clarity about the three aspects related to all five kinds of money. You will receive clarity about what is actually happening and (in my opinion) it will set you up to use one of the greatest mind-body shifting tools, tapping – also known as the Emotional Freedom Technique or EFT. If you have experienced it, you have already felt the power in this technique, or perhaps, you may be in contact with a less effective approach, so the results you got were less than you expected.

In any case, this version of Tapping is <u>very</u>

<u>different</u>. We will be shifting and moving the energy that resides in our nervous system and our body, plus we will be changing the thinking patterns that loop habitually, like some sort of recorded message that plays over and over in our heads. Our Tapping is laser-focused. It will clear and shift what's needed; from the other side of clearing the blocks, we will use it to open up and tap into more energy. This *Personal Wealth Blueprint* is only a starting point in the complete process, but it is a very powerful starting point that will provide you with the necessary clarity and practicality to clear out your main blocks. The recorded version of this exercise can help you to go deeper; you will get it five days after you first subscribe and confirm your subscription (Make sure you use <u>this link,</u> *https://events.genndi.com/register/169105139238 463108/25333aea67)*. My other books, videos, and webinars can assist you to advance further as well.

In any case, we will begin with where you are now, working on your unconscious programming and keeping you on task. The process in front of you is very comprehensive. Its six parts cover everything, from the past that hides most of the set points related to money and wealth, then going forward to discover everything that stops you from having not only more money but also energy: confidence, power, action, focus, decisiveness, etc. We have to be clear about what stops you from being the type of person who stands confidently in your power, creating your life the way you want. There are no instant pushbutton or turnkey solutions. When we apply this process and the money mind-body tool, we start growing and evolving into the version of ourselves that stands tall with more power, more brilliance, and more awesomeness; the people who take more necessary, laser-focused action. We grow into people who easily earn and create wealth. We really want to take you toward a complete process that creates wonder, as I have promised since the beginning of the book. So, let's do it!

Maybe you have already viewed one of my webinars (if so, thank you!), or you may have had some exposure to this approach of clearing blocks to wealth and money. If that is the case, feel free to use your notes in this process of creation of your "Confidential Wealth Blueprint." If this is the first time for you to begin this exercise, now is the time to prepare the first handout we have provided. (If you do not have it, please request the subscription from this link, *https://events.genndi.com/register/169105139238463108/25333aea67,* confirm your subscription and you will get all of the necessary support and materials.) You also have received a second handout, a Tapping script that you can customize based on the work done in this exercise. Your practice sessions will be greatly helped by these tools.

FIVE TYPES OF MONEY

When she began working with multiple clients, Margaret discovered the five kinds of money, particularly when she worked with middle-class clients or those individuals in working-class families. The same thing has been confirmed by many of my colleagues. We have found that, during a general discussion about money or its various related topics (wealth, abundance, prosperity), there is a sort of generalized reaction; as soon as we start to use a specific approach, a much more intensive reaction appears.

As we approach the five aspects of money, we will help you see that there are three pieces of deeper complexity that attach to each of these specific kinds of money.

1) Firs will always be the emotional, nervous-system reactions: feelings, sensations,

anxiety, stress, sadness, and fear. Emotions with the accompanying sensations are literally driven through the autonomic nervous system, until they pop up instantaneously at the very second we start talking specifically about various aspects of money. They're slightly different for each one. Margaret agrees and uses the same word to describe the reaction ("interesting"), because we find it fascinating that our nervous system is wired to instantly react to different aspects of money.

2) Second, there are programmed loops of thinking; Margaret calls them "habitual self-talk." As soon as you start thinking about and working with a certain kind of money, you hear a dialogue in your head of which you probably aren't aware. This process will help you not only to become aware, but also solve the issues connected with these self-talk loops.

This is the sensational thing about self-talk; in a very damaging way, we never question it. These thoughts simply play inside our heads like a recording, over and over, over and over; it is <u>never</u> questioned. We never

ever ask ourselves, "Is this truth?" or "Is this beneficial to me?" We normally reinforce the power of these self-talk loops by listening and allowing them to run throughout our nervous system. For this reason, they are "sensational" in a very bad way. Becoming conscious and aware about habitual self-talk is the real "ah-ha" moment that has the power to create an incredible boost for your advancement. The *Personal Wealth Blueprint* that you will create has the power to transform every aspect of your life.

3) Third, some aspects of money can include an additional important piece: trauma. Although this is not always true, some types of money can be connected to a type of trauma—we call them 'Financial Trauma'. Very often, when tuning into different aspects of money, some sort of dramatic or traumatic experience pops up in your head. That remembrance can be about some type of emotional trauma related to physical issues, relationships, or finances—like when you went bankrupt, or were stolen from, got cheated, or had a battle over money. When you remember the event, you can

say something like, "If that hadn't happened, my financial situation probably wouldn't be like it is today." Usually it will still trigger emotion, so we know it's still active in actually amplifying a nervous system reaction you've already been programmed with.

Now, we're going to focus on four aspects of money, because not everyone has the fifth one. I will explain it a little, but we won't get too far into it. Then we will look at the three aspects under each one.

FIVE TYPES OF MONEY - MAPPING EXERCISE

(Friendly reminder: Before you start, it is warmly recommended that you go through a Connecting to the Source procedure described in the previous chapter.)

Savings

Take out your *Personal Wealth Blueprint* or a piece of paper, and write down the exact amount of money in your savings account right now. (I don't mean in your retirement account or any investments—we are looking at your liquid savings.) If you had an emergency or an unexpected need to repair your car or a household appliance, and you had to pay for it, what is the amount of money that you can tap into easily— what amount do you have in your savings account? Write down that number. This paper is only for you, so be honest with yourself and simply write down the amount of liquid money that you can access easily, in case you need it.

YOU HAVE IT? Okay great.

Take a look at your number, and then take a deep breath.

What thoughts are running through your head right now? Do you hear something going through your head about it, something that you're saying to yourself? Of course, a lot of people will say, "This is not enough, this is not enough money." If you're hearing those types of thoughts in your head (or something similar), I want you to do something that will help you assess how true that feels:

Say these words aloud:

"It's not enough." (Or, you could use the version of the words that you feel is nearer to what you are actually thinking right now; however, these short three words usually are enough).

Say that aloud now, a few times, while looking at the number representing the amount of money in your savings account.

Now, as you look at it and speak it aloud, most times that can increase the intensity of any feeling you're experiencing. Write down what you're feeling on your sheet or paper.

What is blasting through your nervous system, through your head, right now? What is the feeling that you feel? Do you feel something like embarrassment, or more like fear, anger, or frustration? Do you feel a mixture of a few related feelings or opposing feelings? Try to be as honest and defined as possible in this step. Write it down.

Moving on, I would like to ask you about the intensity of those feelings you just defined. Try to define the approximate intensity of what you feel on a scale of 1 to 10. If 10 is the highest possible intensity (like 'I cannot take it anymore') and 1 is the weakest (like 'almost nothing there')—how high is it? Is it a 5? Is it a 7? Or maybe a 3?

Just take your best guess.

Write down the emotion, the feeling, and

whatever you can hear as it runs through your head. Write it down; get it on paper. These are usually quite negative feelings, but do not worry about noticing it, acknowledging it, and writing it down because it will serve your best purpose. Take a minute or two to do that now. (There is no sense in moving on before you do this.) Dig a little bit deeper. You have it? If so, let's move on.

You see, every time you think about your savings, below the level of conscious thought, patterns can pop into our head multiple times a day or week, especially when it is time to pay expenses. What blasts through your nervous system and what runs through your head automatically, without you ever questioning that concept? This is what happens within your mind; I just want you to stop and think about that for a moment. Does that give you a resourceful, empowered state of mind? When you're feeling those emotions, are you feeling enthusiastic and focused on your goals and dreams? Or are you experiencing the 'fight or flight response' and everything that goes with it? (In case you have read clinical descriptions, you would know that this fight-or-flight response narrows your thinking, reduces your resiliency, and prevents you from accessing ideas and inspiration, etc.)

No one enjoys being in a constant state of fight-or-flight response. No one likes spending time with that amount of negative intensity. Think about that for a while. I brought up that topic because I want you to consider having a little more self-compassion right now regarding why your savings might not be exactly where you want them to be; you are probably pretty hard on yourself. Just give yourself a little bit of compassion and understanding. This is why you do not spend enough time creating priorities or strategies that can help; you do not invest needed energy, or seek ideas that can grow your savings account. If your programming says it's impossible to save a lot of money, why would you even try to save it? When you think it's painful or useless or unholy, you won't spend any time on it. Here is your first "ah-ha" moment of this process: give yourself compassion and know that when and *only* when you shift this obstacle, miracles are possible.

Now, what about that third piece for savings?

This may not be relevant to you, but it may be important. When you look at the amount of money in your savings account, is there anything that you're suddenly remembering from the past? Has anything affected your savings today? Write down any reaction like, "It still makes me sad/mad" or "It still feels like such a loss," or "If that hadn't happened, I would have so much more money in my savings account."

Sometimes, an event you remember has nothing to do with money, but it's connected with a feeling. Very often, when people look at their savings, they will feel anxious: "OMG, what if something happens, I have no savings!" That can also bring with it a feeling of sadness or loss, an emotion like this: "I never get to feel entirely safe." Sometimes, a traumatic event from the past involved a sadness or a great loss that made you feel like you lost your security; ever since then, you've never really felt safe. Some people have not felt safe since childhood. Any kind of traumatic event that dramatically changed your life as a child (death of a parent, loss of job, etc) can be connected with this aspect of money called savings. It is most important to understand that savings is both the real amount of money we have, AND an energetic metaphor that translates into is security and safety, a feeling of "I can sleep peacefully now." It may sound a little crazy but when you analyze this, when you really think about it, you'll understand. Savings is a very specific aspect of money; when we have enough of it, we feel safe, and when we don't, we feel very insecure.

Write down any past event that you remember and that fits the previous description. When you think about your savings, it really makes sense that you're feeling everything that you feel right now. You may be feeling anxiety and sadness, loss and frustration, or anger and frustration; whatever you're feeling, it's a reaction to seeing the amount of your savings. (If it's elation, you are blessed!) Despite the reality that is currently manifested in your life, I ask you to understand that the reason your savings are exactly as they are, is because these feelings were there <u>first</u>. You were already wired and programmed with this habitual way of thinking and feeling: "It's not enough. I don't feel safe." That was already there first, at a very unconscious level. It is a clinically proven fact; for those who like to research, feel free to read through materials on the [Stress Project](http://stressproject.org/scientific-research/randomized-control-trials/).

The feelings and the internal wiring of our belief system represent the 'clothing' of our manifested money. We are behaving, thinking, and acting in a way to match our subconscious wiring that determines how things should be and will be for "people like us" (my family, my upbringing, and my social class), the way the world works, and the way money works. Please stay with this idea for a second, because it is important. We received our wiring, and that literally created our money to match these received concepts which matches that wiring!

YES, THIS IS TERRIFYING—FOR MANY OF YOU, IT MAY ALSO BE SHOCKING.

However, this is why clarity is so wonderful. The start of great changes happen once you realize, "My gosh, we can change everything!" Once you see the root of the problem that has caused you so much suffering, and even more importantly, when you learn how to use this powerful tool of Tapping, all of a sudden you understand how to create a whole new reality in your savings. It's simply amazing. It's powerful.

We just have to get through the difficult part of seeing it and getting through all these strong emotions. The upcoming process of shifting and accepting them will move them, and through Tapping, we can get to the other side. And I promise you, that's what we will do.

Debt

We can move out of the second element; though it will be faster, in a sense it will also get worse because we're going to work with your amount of debt. In case you're one of those lucky ones who do not have any debt, just visualize anyone else who has debt, and feel grateful that this important aspect of money is missing from your *Personal Wealth Blueprint*. Serious issues are hidden within this aspect of money for many people, but even if you have no debt, it might be worthwhile to work through this issue. Perhaps you have constant anxiety about debt, or you're super debt-averse and you can't tolerate any debt at all. Any area where you have a big emotional response, you will want to work on that. I know people who have no debt, but they're so afraid of having debt that it stops them from even getting into good or necessary debt, because they are panicking to pay everything off. They live a very hand-to-mouth form of existence. They have exchanged debt with anxiety about having debt. In many cases, that can be the same problem or even worse.

Write down how much debt you have. The real, total amount of debt.

What we are after is troublesome debt, like credit card debt or any other bad debt. Do not necessarily count your good debt at this point, like a mortgage or a necessary business loan. This is the place to summarize the amount of debt that is triggering an emotional response that you don't feel good about. For example, some people feel fantastic about their school loans because the loans allow them to work on a job with great pay. On other hand, some people feel extremely upset about their school loans—they feel tricked, cheated, and treated unfairly.

What piece of your debt is upsetting to you? We're looking to find the yucky stuff and work with that, so take a minute to list those amounts on a piece of paper. Notice if you're already starting to have a feeling about it.

Now, write down any *feelings or emotions* that are blasting through your head while looking at that number in front of you. Are there any words that you're saying about yourself, about money and wealth, about the world, about the way things are? What words or phrases are running through your head as you look at the total amount of your debt? Be introspective here, as much you can. These ideas are sometimes hard to catch since this works on autopilot and you don't even question it.

These are some common examples:

- "No matter what I do, I can never get ahead."
- "What I do is never enough."
- "I'm a loser."
- "I'm a failure."
- "It's impossible to get out of this."
- "The cards are stacked against me."
- "It's going to be hard if even possible…"
- "I'll never get out from under this."
- "How could I even come to this?"

These kinds of thoughts move through our heads on a daily basis. Just like our savings, often anxiety is the emotion immediately triggered, with debt as the number-one reason for the emotion of shame (or embarrassment, a more socially accepted form of shame). You can be sure that shame is one of the most powerfully negative emotions that you could ever possibly experience. Seriously, what's worse than shame? Panic at life-threatening levels can be extremely uncomfortable, but shame is even more damaging since we experience it a lot, sometimes all day long, multiple times a day, depending on how you've been programmed to feel shame.

As with savings, how much time and energy do we spend on solving this issue in an effective way? We know that there are amazing financial advisors, planners, CPAs, and accountants who can help; there are books and strategies on debt reduction that can help. But consider, from the amount of your energy, focus, and attention that you bring to your day job, how much do you think you spend on actually dealing with your own debt? Especially if every time you think about it, that debt triggers a wall of shame and really negative inner talk.

CAUTION: While considering money that we owe to others, we are usually so negative and hard on ourselves! I want to ask you to please, show yourself a tiny bit of compassion <u>right now</u>. Allow a tiny bit of compassion and understanding that you are not in a resourceful state. Margaret explains (and I share that experience) that when working through this process with financial advisors, CPAs, and all sorts of money experts (i.e. bankers who are incredibly brilliant at advising other people about their debt), toward their own debt, they're often stuck in a disaster zone. They get busy avoiding it, they get frozen in fear, they're in shame—believe me, it's not just you who goes through negative cycles about money.

Lastly, this can be a big block: Has a past event really affected your debt, something that causes you look back and say, "If that hadn't happened..."?

As coaches, we have found that, if there is a connected trauma to debt, it often involves some sort of betrayal, something that you've never forgiven yourself or someone else for. In any case, you haven't forgiven yourself, because when you look back over your history, it affected you financially. Maybe that was a bad decision or something about what you are saying to yourself: "I should've known better. I was an idiot. I should've been smarter." That is very common when people look at their debt.

It may be similar within the courthouse inside of your head, the place where you are judging yourself every day and saying, "I was an idiot, I was so stupid," etc. When people are stuck in that mode of being unable to be forgiven (and people can remain there for 20 or up to 50 years), they haven't had a good way to process that. Tapping is an incredible way to process a past event. We actually work in-depth with Financial Trauma issues; my next book will cover this subject in a deeper way, but at this point, you will get a way to release and shift what is needed at the start.

Now, let's say you don't have a good way to process it so that it is cleared out from your system, so that you can come back to self-compassion, self-forgiveness, and understanding. You need to get rid of all the programs running on repeat mode in these ways: "I was an idiot. I should've known better. I should have done better. It's all my fault. Every time I look at my debt, I think, 'I'm an idiot, I'm a loser, I'm a failure.'" This translates into, "I deserve to be punished. I deserve what I'm getting." These programs need to go.

I've seen people hold onto debt unconsciously, with all of their actions lining up in an elegant, sophisticated way to ensure that they always remain in debt; it's self-punishment because they've never forgiven themselves. I'm going to ask again: Every time you look at your debt, are you using this debt as self-punishment? Or are you using this debt as a reminder that you were wronged in the past, and you've never been able to make it right? Just like the savings account, debt is dollars and cents in the real world; it's also an energetic or emotional metaphor for punishing yourself or punishing someone else by saying, "Look what you did to me." This is really important to see and understand.

We often ask people, "When you look at your debt, how would you finish this sentence? "That means I'm '_____'."

People almost always fill in the blank with something dark and negative, such as, "a failure, a loser." In translation, "This debt means I'm always failing, or not good enough, or a loser." It's never positive. So if that's how people have lived their lives, if that's the habitual self-talk coming out in them, of course they create debt because it's a self-fulfilling loop of punishment. It is filled with phrases like these: "I should have known better; I should be smarter,." It actually means, "I need to learn a lesson. I need this punishment to remind me—to be my lesson."

Please, look at your debt again and ask yourself if you have *suffered enough,* if you have *tortured yourself enough over it*. Now please, get ready to move forward with energy. Take a breath and move into a new chapter where you don't need to be punished every time the money topic appears.

Income

As you will see, the next two topics are very closely related. We are switching gears! As soon as these are covered, we will apply Tapping in a very customized and personalized way. But before moving on to income, let's go back to your *Personal Wealth Blueprint* or piece of paper; write down a ballpark amount of your monthly expanses. Now, write down your monthly earnings, your income. It's important to find out how much is left after paying bills. If you are not sure, simply write down your best guess.

Now, stay on that page for a few moments, and look at this amount of money. What are you saying and feeling about this amount of money; what comes up? In this step, people will often hear, "It's not enough, it's just not enough!" If you are hearing something like that or anything similar, can you describe the feeling you have? Check your income number again, or what is left of it. Do you feel, "It is NOT enough?" Say the words out loud; "IT IS NOT ENOUGH" (or as you hear it in your head). Repeat it again. What are the feelings and emotions? Capture everything you hear in your head, the feelings and emotions streaming through your system <u>now</u>.

Also, if you start remembering something from

your past that's connected with earning, take note of it; something that made you feel strong negative emotions may indicate a connected trauma. That may be anything that made you feel ashamed, sad, or scared; perhaps a parent had a devastating event happen to their income. Many people remember life-altering instances, such as a parent's financial crisis, relocation, or something as small as parent(s) stopping their allowance. These are just a few examples.

What shows up right here and now is unconscious programming around your sense of value and worth, based on your family upbringing, tradition, or origin. Phrases like "People like us," "In our family," or "This is how much we earn" equates with "This is how much we're worth. We're the Joneses or the Millers; we're not those people over there who earn a lot of money."

Other phrases might include, "We work hard, we get screwed, the government and/or the tax man is against us—the little guys." These sets of beliefs really depend on your upbringing and early impressions related to earnings, business, and wealth. Some beliefs would keep you stuck on certain income levels for years, or make you spend more than you should; some would push you to earn the same or even less than your parents, living paycheck to paycheck. Because you see the holes and mismatch in the reality around you, your thoughts might shift in this direction: "I want to earn well," "I need more money," "I have to advance my business," or "I should have more from life." Your thoughts may get even louder in the next section regarding Income Goals, because that's like saying, "Now I'm going to go much higher." At an income level, we see the pushback from our programming about what is possible for us to earn and what we deserve, based on our inner programming about our value. Often when we look at our income, when it's not enough, we hear things in our head; we feel anxiety, or sometimes a sadness or a frustration, like "No matter what I do…"

Sometimes the self-talk will sound like this: "I'm not earning enough. I'm not enough. I'm not valuable enough. People don't value me enough."

Income Goal

As we switch over to this Income Goal section, we turn up the heat a bit; that's why this most necessary section holds great value. Every single one of you would say, "I would really love to double or even triple my income, Sasha!" In reply, I would say that it sounds good in theory but as a matter of fact, the second we write it on paper, it starts to feel differently. So, let's do that. Get your paper and write down a big goal for your income. What would you love to earn? For this purpose, I don't want you to break yourself stretching toward some huge, unreasonable (for you) income goal like $2 million or $5 million, at least not right away. The best thing is to write the next number just above where you are now, so that it feels realistic despite being a step up. Maybe that next income goal is to double your current monthly earnings. Make it one step up, not all the way to the multi-millions, because there's something about reaching toward the millions that creates a feeling of disassociation for most people; you won't really feel anything about it, neither will it serve your purpose.

So, write down your next step up. Now, take a look at the number; at first, some people will feel excited, but we are interested in the other side of it. Sure, the excitement is what we want, what drives us forward. There is always a side of you that tends to think, "Infinite possibilities, yes! Anything's possible!" We don't have to take power from that side of you; it's great! What we do want is to clear the inner skeptic side of you, the one that holds all of the programming that we don't normally see or hear very clearly. We're going to let in the inner skeptic and invite him to speak freely, for a time; we need to see what's pushing back in our system.

Again, it's fantastic that you have an enthusiastic and positive side; we don't want to mess with that, but you also have an inner skeptic that slows you down and battles you almost all the time. So, let's say you were to look at that Income Goal you have just written down, and say aloud, **"It's impossible!"** This statement allows the inner skeptic to speak, to see how true it feels. Say that phrase again. **"It's impossible!"** Where is it on a scale of 1 to 10 (one as 100% easily possible and 10 as totally impossible)? Most people will hover somewhere around 6 or 7; what is your number? Which emotion gets triggered when looking for this answer? What is the emotion you feel right now? Is it a feeling of, "Wow, me earning this amount per month is impossible"?

Sometimes the inner critic sounds something like this:

- "It would probably be really hard."
- "I'd have to work all the time."
- "I'd never see my kids………….."
- "I wouldn't have time to relax or meditate…."
- "I will not have time to exercise or do all the things I really like to do."
- "It would be terrible and painful; I would hate my life."

Remember, with the help of your inner skeptic/critic right now, we're revealing your paradigm; this programming says, "Based on my value, this is how hard I have to work for my money." This is a really crucial point.

As soon as you set a bigger goal, it's almost like saying, "If I am so valuable, in order to get to this goal or earn this much money, I will have to work twice as hard, and put in twice as many hours." Part of our brain already knows that other people don't work twice as hard to get paid much more, and it knows there are ways of leveraging, outsourcing, up-selling, getting more or better clients (i.e. **getting paid more**). However, your inner skeptic (that holds this paradigm together) will say something like this. *"It's going to be really hard. You'll never see your kids; it's going to be hellish,"* etc.

Margaret Lynch and other expert Tapping Into Wealth coaches, including me, have seen people cry after looking at a big goal and saying, "I want to believe in the universe and the Law of Attraction; I do write down my goals." Next they start to feel sad: "It's really impossible for me. I don't want to suffer, working like a dog without seeing my kids. It's so sad because I really want this but there's no way to do it." Gradually, they get rid of that goal. Margaret explains:

"I've had friends who've come into workshops that I've done, buddies I worked with for years in corporate, and watch them through the course of the workshop, erase the goal and make it smaller and smaller and smaller. This is how I learned I had to do this around Income Goals. I thought, "Why is everyone making the goal smaller every day that goes by?" Because the more they looked at it, the worse they felt. That feeling of "It's impossible" made them feel awful.

I really would like you to consider this one main thing. If you're an achiever who loves to create, if you're smart and know how to get things done, to have a goal that feels impossible – that you have no idea how to reach—that goal will make you feel demoralized. And it would be insane to spend any time or effort to put your heart into running after a goal that quite frankly, feels impossible! If you look at this from another angle, that is the *definition of insanity*: investing time, energy, and effort into the pursuit of something that feels 100% impossible. Even if it feels 50% impossible, it simply doesn't make sense. From this point of view, I hope you can better see why this is really important to hear, to have clarity about what pushes back inside of you, and the feelings and emotions that arise.

The connected goal trauma is a very specific thing. Once you look at the numbers and consider your income goal, lots of feelings and emotions run through your head, blasting through your nervous system; sometimes there is a connected trauma (that Margaret has discovered) based on the experience of working with thousands of people. Sometimes people have set a really big goal in the past that they really believed in; they worked really hard, moved heaven and earth, and nearly killed themselves—maybe they even destroyed their health in going for that goal—and it didn't work out. This issue (of goal trauma and financial trauma) will be covered in an entirely separate book, just like we can do in private, one-on-one coaching sessions.

For many people, Goal Trauma and Financial Trauma come up as serious blockages and obstacles for advancement and gaining freedom from pre-programmed limiting paradigms. Be sure that if you have one of those, it will hang over your head like a dark cloud until something disperses it.

Toxic Money

This form of money is not present in everyone's reality; however, if it is present, you really have to know about it and start clearing it out because it works like an octopus. Toxic Money involves a situation where you either owed money or received money owed to you, and it came with a battle; perhaps it's being withheld from you. This can also be money that you did receive, but it came with a big price tag attached, and you're still angry about it; you're still holding a grudge. This money becomes toxic because from the moment it became soured by association, you won't be able to earn more. Over and over, we hear from people's experiences. They'll say something like this: "From the moment I went to battle around this time or because of this money, somehow I've never been able to earn again. I lost my job, and then this other thing happened and this other thing happened; literally, I haven't been able to earn at all—or earn more than a very small amount."

The other area where Toxic Money can play out is when you receive money from someone (partner, friend, elderly parent), but that relationship isn't really a healthy one. Sometimes the person(s) can be paying for some part of your lifestyle, bailing you out in a way, and it's money that you really need, yet you hate taking it. It comes at a price. You are stuck or disempowered, or a little bit in victim mode and need to be rescued, and there's something about the money that you both need and yet can't stand at the same time. See how that's toxic? It's like an octopus because that money looks like the issue, but the issue is really wrapped up in all of the relationship struggles, all of the battle-related, power-disempowerment elements—taking away and needing and demanding and refusing.

So, Toxic Money is a little more complicated. If you have it, this can be a great "ah-ha" moment. It does a very particular type of shutdown on your capacity for growth, but the work on it is more like navigating through a maze, because it involves working through all of the related relationship elements. With this '*Shortcut to Having More*' method, you will definitely approach the roots of this problem, but to know how to deal with this successfully, you really need more. Personal coaching will easily clear the Toxic Money problem, but sometimes a good effort is needed because of its specific nature. If you want to actually work with somebody who is qualified and knows this work inside and out, I strongly recommend that, especially if you detect any traces of Toxic Money. You can approach me and my team through my website or look for a qualified person elsewhere; I always recommend trained Tapping into Wealth Coaches.

Personal Wealth Blueprint Tapping Script

Look at your *Personal Wealth Blueprint* sheet again. Look at all of the things you've written down about money—all the different numbers and parts—and please tune in to the present moment, to whatever feeling you noted down. It may be something related to embarrassment and shame, most probably a phrase like this: "God, it's so uncomfortable; it's embarrassing. I'm so ashamed," if you have dug down enough. Or probably something that sounds like this: "I'm such a loser." That's also shame in disguise. And there are other feelings you noted down. Use the provided

Personal Wealth Blueprint Tapping Script handout to create a personalized Tapping Script. That is very important; soon it will really serve your purpose with great power and significance.

CLEARING

Preparation

Since so many people carry inside of them different programming, experiences, histories and issues, as soon as we start with a tapping exercise, we will address the biggest issues that come up for most people. However, the unique point about this method is a fact that this is a customized practice, constructed in the best way to serve your own needs. Tapping has been around for a while now. If you have already done some tapping before, but you didn't experience strong enough results, I can just repeat what I already told you: the approach offered here is a lot different than most of the heavily promoted tapping schools and methodologies.

In our process, for example, the way to get to the other side is to accept all feelings. We are going to tap, voice, and move the energy. Our approach to Tapping is very different; it successfully shifts the person to the other side of negative elements.

It is an incredible and clinically proven PTSD tool, so it works fantastically on all of the emotions that you may be carrying, about any past traumatic events.

In order to maximize the efficiency of the clearing process while Tapping, basically two (uncomplicated) things must be done:

- If you haven't done any tapping before, you will have to familiarize yourself with a simple method of tapping.
- Prepare your personalized Tapping Script.

Once you request the materials from [our link here](), *https://events.genndi.com/register/169105139238463108/25333aea67,* you will receive a video that shows you a practical way to apply our version of Tapping, and another handout named, "The Tapping Script – Customized from Your Personal Wealth Blueprint". You can print out this script and then fill in the blanks. It takes introspection but it's very easy to do. Literally, you fill in the most intense emotions that appear in you, that came out in your Money Map. You can actually plug in very personal, specific items and use that as your homework.

I want you to make a commitment to really do this Tapping. If you want to make a change in your money, it starts with this inner shift, and Tapping is a really powerful, helpful tool. It will shift you every time. Right now, we want to get you rewired so that when you deal with any of the five kinds of money, you are in a highly resourceful state rather than a negative, drained, habitual state. That comes from your programming, which you don't really want to be in and never really chose to be in, right? No one chose to act this way around money!

We want to lead you out of that path, and it's going to take some commitment. I recommend that you give it a minimum of 21 days' commitment before you work through the next book, the next customized Tapping Script, or even personal coaching. Really tap through this script at least once every 48 hours. Literally, it will take few minutes per day to do it, and it will make a massive difference in your overall stress response around money. If after three weeks you cannot feel a significant shift and change, I would be greatly surprised. If that happens to you, simply ask for a refund and you will get it, no questions asked!

I typically use these Tapping points:

Eyebrow point

Side of the Eye point

Under the Eye point

Under the Nose point

Chin point (in the cleft of the chin)

Collarbone point (very good to use when emotions get more intense or when you feel the word session or Tapping session reaching deeper)

Top of the Head point

Under the Armpit point (although not always practical, use it any time you can)

There are more Tapping points, such as the karate-chop point or the side-of-the-hand point. You can see all of these on the image or by looking at different tapping videos, books, etc. However, it's not necessary to do all of the points. There is nothing magical about any particular tapping point;

please keep that in mind.

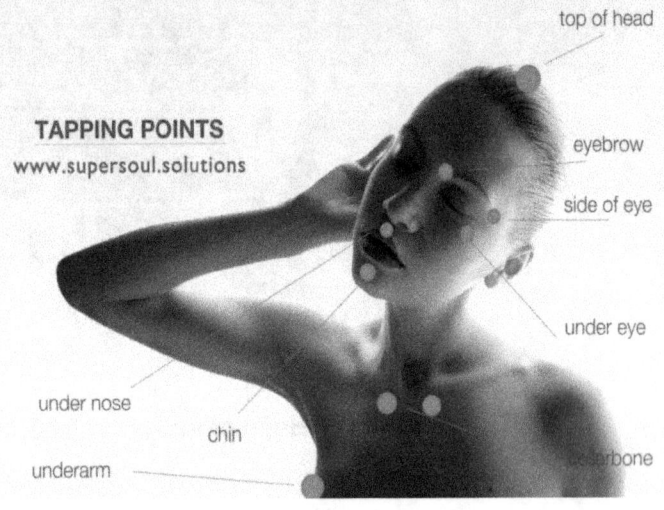

Generally, tapping has been around since the 1980s. It has worked in the same way; it's never really varied. We should tap on enough points to generate a strong current for shifting the nervous system. All of these are acupuncture points, clinically proven to shift or turn off, or (to use clinical term) "down-regulate" the autonomic nervous system; we're not just randomly tapping our body. When we tap and voice negative things, negative words, negative beliefs, and negative feelings, they don't get stronger; they actually get lighter and weaker. When we release them, the inner skeptic gets calmer and all the negative self-talk starts feeling less true.

BECAUSE OF THAT, YOU SHOULD NEVER WORRY ABOUT TAPPING AND SAYING SOMETHING THAT MIGHT SOUND REALLY NEGATIVE—EVEN OVER-THE-TOP NEGATIVE. IT ACTUALLY WORKS BETTER TO JUST GET IT OUT OF YOUR WHOLE BODY AND NERVOUS SYSTEM.

When you get inside the tapping practice, you'll find relief. The negative words stop feeling true anymore; they stop wasting your energy and misguiding your thoughts, attention, and action. The exact sequence you use is also unimportant, or the number of times you tap each point. We tend to tap four or five times on each point. Just move through the points at your own pace. You will get phrases to say out loud (or repeat them after me, if you are using guided audio)—you can be as loud as you want. Maybe if you're in public, you might want to mumble. You just need to stimulate the acupuncture points enough to make a shift in the nervous system. And believe me, you'll feel it.

DIGGING ROUND

In this section, I will provide you with the Tapping Script that, according to experience collected from working with hundreds and thousands of clients, is more than effective as a first round of Tapping, an opening "Digging Round". Start with this script, then work with the next "Positive Round," and lastly with your own script that's been customized to your own needs and situation.

Of course, I want you to get as many benefits and results as you can, in the shortest amount of time possible. For that reason, I repeat the request for you to not rely only on the power of these two scripts. That both digging and positive rounds are powerful and important, there is no doubt; however, you will get even more benefits once you create and start using your personalized Tapping Script, with the help of a handout that you received with the other materials. The whole process starts here; I will send you recording and materials that will help and support you to adjust and learn this process in a practical and easy way. So let's start right away.

Start with any of the Tapping points – just jump right in and repeat after me:

It's overwhelming

It's overwhelming

Every part of my money

And I'm feeling it

I'm feeling it

It's so heavy

All through my body

I'm so ashamed

It's so wrong

It's so embarrassing

And it's so scary

All this shame in my body

All this stress in my nervous system

It's overwhelming

No wonder I don't spend a lot of time thinking about my money

All this guilt

God I'm such a loser

Failure

Failure in money

I'm so ashamed

I'm just going to accept that heavy feeling

Shame, shame, shame

Stuck in my stomach

Like a pit

And what if it never changes?

It's so awful and scary

I feel so awful

All this shame

I accept everything I feel

SHORTCUT TO HAVING MORE

I've said this to myself a million times

Failure

Shameful

Frustrating

It's depressing

I'm disappointed in myself

I should be doing better

I should know better

I should make different choices

I should be able to figure this out

And I never do

I can never get ahead

Failure

So heavy

I accept all of these dark feelings

I accept that I've been carrying them

And maybe even my parents carried them

All of these dark, shameful feelings

I've made so many mistakes

Don't I deserve to yell at myself?

If anyone saw these numbers

I'd be so embarrassed

Horrified and mortified

And people would see the truth about me

That I'm an idiot

Or I'm not strong enough

Or I'm missing something

People would judge me

And, oh, I judge myself

All of this shame

I've been telling myself

That I deserve to feel bad

And I'm just going to accept that

I've been really hard on myself

Torturing myself really

Don't I deserve to feel ashamed?

Look at these numbers!

Don't I deserve to beat myself up?

To judge myself harshly?

I've been judging myself for years

Feeling ashamed

And from that place

Everything feels impossible

And overwhelming

And I'm just going to accept that

I accept this feeling of shame

This self-punishment

And I'm open to lightening it up

Maybe it's time

All this shame in my body

All this shame about money

Shame about earning

Shame about spending

Shame that I don't earn enough

I literally can't win

I accept everything I'm feeling

And I'm open to light

Compassion

Healing

The truth is

I've seen things today

In a whole new light

I get it

Maybe it's time

To let go of some of this shame

To let go of my long history of self-punishment

Maybe it's time

I can't move forward without it

And I really do want to move forward

Anxiety in my body about money

Deep programming, fear, and anxiety about money

Anxiety wired into my nervous system

And the thoughts I think over and over

I totally accept them

And I'm open to healing

For my highest good.

Now take a deep breath.

It's always good to take a cleansing breath after a long round of Tapping like that. I want you to check something right after Tapping. Sometimes as we tap, we'll begin the process with a feeling that will rise to a peak and then increase (i.e. get worse), and then start to weaken and settle. So just as a check-in—what feeling is left? Is it still shame, or anxiety? Or is there a mixture of compassion? Remember that when you're feeling shame (embarrassment), it simply means there is a process going on in you energetically, emotionally, unconsciously—at every level—that says, "I don't deserve (something good)." Or said another way, "I deserve exactly what I'm getting (something bad)."

When you shift toward and nurture at least a bit of self-compassion, that's like a quantum leap because this is what that really sounds and feels like. Close your eyes and take a breath as I describe the meaning of self-compassion:

"Oh, my God, I've been doing my best. I actually deserve better than this. I deserve a hug and some compassion, and some consideration. And I deserve to feel better. I deserve happiness. I deserve some joy."

Do you see how different that sounds, from "I deserve this c*ap" to "I actually deserve better, and I think I'm ready to receive that"? It's arising from that unconscious place, that drives everything that you manifest, every action that you take. That aligns your brilliance, your focus, and your energy with your actions.

This will change you, and it will change what the Universe brings to you. If you're running this sort of internal program, "I deserve to feel ashamed; I'm an idiot; I'm stupid; I created this mess; It's all my fault," then this is what you're really saying to the Universe: "Keep punishing me, please, because that's what I'm resonating." When you say, "I actually deserve some compassion and some joy," you're no longer saying, "Keep punishing me." And I'm telling you, if you have been mixing in punishment with your money story that says, "I don't deserve a lot (i.e. your income or savings account)," when you start shifting inside, everything will change – even your debt.

At times, when compassion starts to open up, sometimes it triggers sadness. Place your hand on your heart and say, "I've been so hard on myself. I've literally broken my own heart." Because that's exactly what happens when you're this hard on yourself, when a recorded voice in your head is saying, "I'm an idiot; I'm a loser; It's all my fault; It's not enough; I'm not good enough..." over and over again. You're breaking your own heart on a subtle plane. Just close your eyes and place your hand on your heart for a second, and see if some understanding floods in, based on all the "ah-ha" moments you have received today.

POSITIVE ROUND

There is still more work to do. The fact is that your nervous system has run in that programmed way for a really long time. Naturally, it will take some time to rewire that habitual programmed response, but this is the way we start: *compassion and willingness*.

We're going to finish up with another round of Tapping, a more positive round. Let's go back to the Tapping points again, you know how to do them:

I've been really hard on myself

And it's been really hard on me

To have this much negative programming in my money

To feel like things are disappointing and impossible

To feel like the cards are stacked against me

That's some really hard stuff

To feel like I don't have enough value or worth to earn more

To feel powerless and disappointed in money all the time

That's hard

I've lived with anxiety and shame for years

I've paid a real price for my programming

It's hard stuff

And I carry it 24 hours a day

Sometimes it wakes me up in the middle of the night

And I can't sleep

Worrying about money

I totally honor myself

And I've added on top of that

Being really hard on myself

Really mean

Actually mean to myself

I've added to this

Being ruthless

Ruthlessly critical of myself

To the point that I've broken my own heart before

I've literally beaten myself down

Of course that's showing up in my money

And maybe I have insight on why I do that

But either way

I'm just going to accept it in a new light today

I give myself the gift of compassion

I give myself the gift of understanding

I'm opening my heart

The wisdom of my heart

And understanding

All of this

At a higher level

This is so much bigger than money

And it's really affecting my money

I give myself the gift

Of self-love

And the reminder

Or the new information

That I do deserve

I deserve happiness

I deserve to feel safe

I've never gotten that

And I have a lot of grief about that

And whenever I look at my money

It's just a giant metaphor

I have a lot of sadness

And I'm just going to honor that

I accept the sadness

Because it's accepting me

And everything I've lost

Because of the shame and the fear

Because of this programming I have around money

And because I love myself so much

I am going to heal this

I honor myself now

I honor who I am and who I've always been

And I honor who I am becoming

In these 90 minutes, I've become more conscious and more compassionate

And that is HUGE

I honor who I'm becoming

Conscious and deserving when it comes to money

Powerful and resourceful when it comes to money

And I bless everything I wrote down on this piece of paper

I bless all of these numbers

It's my current reality

It's what I've created based on my entire life of programming

I'm doing my best

And everything's changing now

I bless my current reality

And I am open

To everything that is now possible and unfolding for me

I commit to holding this compassion for myself in my heart

Over the next week

And saying a new thing in my head

Which is this:

I deserve better

I deserve more

I want more

And I deserve it

Take a deep breath...

Just try to feel what is happening in your body now. There should be quite a lot of energy movement. Even over the next 24 hours, these rounds of Tapping will act on, integrate, and reorganize your subconscious mind, your unconscious mind, and your nervous system. This, my dear friends, is literally changing your inner conditioned wiring; the exact nature of what has stopped you from Having More will start to melt right here. The end isn't here, but it is a fantastic beginning. To shift the wiring in your nervous system, it's all about **neuroplasticity** - we need to do both: detect the issue, and remove that stuff.

That turns down the old reaction. We need to proactively put in some new things like the words, "I deserve better, I actually deserve more, " and compassion—holding compassion in your heart, for yourself, to begin to see the bigger picture. Everything in an even more accelerated way will happen when you use your personalized Tapping

Script.

Personal Wealth Blueprint Tapping Script

If you didn't do it until now, please take a look at your *Personal Wealth Blueprint* sheet again, or at the notes you took instead of using the provided sheet. Look at all of the numbers and parts you've written down about money; please tune in to the present moment, to whatever feelings you noted down. Something in relation to embarrassment and shame; if you have dug deep enough, it's most probably a phrase like this: "God, it's so uncomfortable, it's embarrassing I'm so ashamed." Or probably something that sounds like this: "I'm such a loser." That's also shame in disguise. No doubt, there are other feelings you noted down. Use the provided *Personal Wealth Blueprint* Tapping Script handout to create a personalized tapping script. That is very important; you have to start using it. After you worked with the previously provided Tapping Scripts, you are now ready go even deeper. You already feel the power of the process. By now, I am sure you do.

Now, once you start working with your *Personal Wealth Blueprint* Tapping Script, you will further accelerate your transformation and growth. You can continue using the previously provided scripts but you *Personal Wealth Blueprint* will just hit your conditioning better. Use it every other day or every day; mix it with 'digging' and 'positive' tapping rounds as you feel is best. While working in that way, you will create an immensely positive response of your nervous system and subconscious mind. As explained previously, all these methods in the scripts will serve your purpose with great power and significance. As soon you start applying this correctly, you will feel the energy moving quickly.

SHORTCUT TO HAVING MORE

CONCLUDING WORDS

If you really think about what we are doing with all of this tapping and clearing, you will see the formation of a brand-new way of operating. I had you say these words: "I commit to my better future. I commit to holding this compassion for myself in my heart." I had you say something new: "I deserve better; I deserve to have and become more." Why did I do that? Because from that energy, from that place, everything is possible. It's just what we need in order to get unstuck and move quickly towards our goals.

In one area, people sometimes get confused: it may happen that after Tapping, you might feel a little low-energy, a little tired or lightheaded, but there is no reason to worry. Most people do not have these symptoms, but if you do, keep in mind that is a normal state that we have to get through. We do a LOT with this process. Just consider it as a draining process, even if you do not feel that way, because we're dredging really heavy stuff. We're voicing it, accepting it, and moving it. You may have more tears to cry for yourself, and that's okay; cry those tears for yourself, don't keep them inside. Let those tears flow for yourself, because that sadness is accepting you. But I promise that on the other side of moving this dark, heavy stuff, you're opening up a storehouse of energy, focus, and determination; this activity will change every aspect of your money.

It takes a lot of energy to hold back all of these things! Keeping old programming active in us wastes a lot of energy. It makes us do all sorts of things we do not really want or even need; specifically, it makes us move toward really non-beneficial behavior and activities in relation to money.

IT'S SUCH A WASTE OF TIME, THIS UNCONSCIOUS PROGRAMMING. IT MAKES YOU DO ALL SORTS OF CRAZY THINGS AND AFFECTS YOUR MONEY, WITHOUT YOU EVEN REALIZING IT.

When we clear these unwanted blocks,

everything transmutes to a more focused, more conscious, and more creative you. On the other hand, this process is demanding and it goes deep. Therefore, if you feel overly intense emotions or no emotions (or emotions that are too weak), simply let yourself process over the next few days, then go back to your routine. It may be hard or feel heavy, but keep Tapping! This is a major event happening inside of you; know that you will get to the other side because Tapping works.

I want to close this book by saying that I'm so happy for you and proud of you for being here. I honor what you have started on this journey with me, and I honor you for jumping in and 'taking the chance'. Some of you know me; some of you have never heard of me until now. In any case, be sure that if you continue this work with me, we get deeper with each step. I am very serious as well as dedicated about getting specific and clearing your money blocks. I am honored to be doing this with you. Do your homework. Do the Tapping as described in the book and support materials (if you still did not, please get them from [this link](https://events.genndi.com/register/169105139238463108/25333aea67), *https://events.genndi.com/register/169105139238463108/25333aea67*). I hope I will see you in part two of this journey.

Feel free to visit my website, and contact me with any questions. At the end, I need to clear something that I see many people retain because they are either hiding or misunderstanding. It's about the myth of instant results. This is a really powerful *beginning of the process* but it's not the end. There are no pushbutton or instant solutions that are worthy of your time, at least not in this arena.

Reality Check

Since we are nearing the end (of the beginning), this reality check is probably most important to note. For those who will not give this practice a chance, nothing I promised you can happen. Since it's a really easy and immensely important process, please do not turn it into another 'virtual dust collector', collecting piles of dead data on your hard drive. As soon as you start applying it, you will feel better and gain greater improvements. However, though this is not a negative, I will not keep you from the truth—this cannot be the end of your journey.

I sincerely hope that you recognize this point as just the beginning. Not everyone can immediately afford to work with a personal Tapping into Wealth Coach or another professional who is really able to help. Some people think that personal coaching on this level is an immensely high-priced service, which is not true. Of course, this personal one-on-one work cannot be sold for just any amount; however, people usually think that the personal care of a qualified Tapping into Wealth and/or Transformational expert costs much more than it actually does. When working together and under the care of a personal coach leading you through the labyrinth of connections between pre-programmed patterns, limiting beliefs, habitual self-talk, and traumatic money-related experiences, you have the best and fastest way to advance energy results quickly.

In that way, you are near to getting clear of everything that hinders your progress to earning and keeping more money. Releasing any limits on your way to having more and becoming more is priceless; the same is not true for any type of guidance. However, the guidance of a qualified coach who can really shorten your struggles cannot be defined with a price tag, since it is based on the results you get from it; you will achieve limitless financial capacity. When the lion is released from its cage, nobody can stop it. When an eagle breaks free, who can bring it back into captivity?

Despite the fact that personal coaching does not carry a six-digit hourly price, I am well aware that many people will still be unable (not only due to financial reasons) to afford a good and qualified expert. For that reason, I will continue publishing upcoming parts of this comprehensive approach to Having More and becoming more. Using these means, I really feel I have done my best to share this most valuable, no B.S., direct, and efficient way that saved me from staying on the bottom; I have also shared this with many more individuals outside of my clients and personal students.

If you have any further questions or enquiries, feel free to contact me and my team members on [my website](http://supersoul.solutions/) (http://supersoul.solutions/) or [Facebook page](https://www.facebook.com/supersoul.solutions/) (https://www.facebook.com/supersoul.solutions/).

You can email me and my team via supersoul.solutions_at_gmail.com; our usual response time is 48 hours.

Wishing you all the best with full success, fast clearing, growth, and the achievement of all your desires.

Sasha James

If you prefer, in order to get support materials you can use this QR code:

Check out the author's Amazon profile here,
https://www.amazon.com/Sasha-James/e/B01NBS76A3/

Next Steps

Please, consider writing an honest review about this book. I truly value your opinion and thoughts, and I will incorporate them into my next book, which is already being prepared.

Leave your review of my book on the Kindle Page.

Wishing you all the best with full success, fast clearing, growth, and the achievement of all your goals and desires.

THANK YOU!

More Great and Helpful Books Authored

By Sasha James *and* Sifu William Lee

Author of Amazon Bestsellers:

5-Minute Chi Boost

5- Minute Stress Management

Healing Chi Meditation

Qigong Meridian Self Massage

Chi Healing Powers Book Set

&

Total Chi Fitness

All Rights Reserved 2017 @POWER of ONE

www.ingramcontent.com/pod-product-compliance
Lightning Source LLC
Chambersburg PA
CBHW061436180526
45170CB00004B/1436